The P.R.I.S.M. Salvation

A 3-Step Solution
to Social Media Domination
for Busy Business Owners

By: Mike Saunders, MBA

Table of Contents

Chapter 1
Before The Story

"Dreams meet reality only when someone shows the courage to accept challenges"

We all have dreams but seldom do we have what it takes to back them with our courage to accept the challenges necessary to succeed. Thus, most of our dreams keep on maintaining their *status quo*! The ones who dare to walk the extra mile are the real winners.

After completing my MBA in Marketing, I realized that so much of what we all as consumers today experience in being "marketed to," is rooted in the basic foundation of marketing theories of marketing strategy. But it hit me: so much of social media marketing is done wrong! I see people attempting to take advantage of various social media tools to make a quick buck and are making a nuisance of themselves in the process.

Social media was never intended for that and if you can learn the principles discussed in this book you will never make those mistakes. Integrating an MBA-level marketing strategy with social media tools will give your message the power it needs to be properly delivered to your prospects.

I think when we all first heard the term "internet marketing," it was just a new way to sell things online that no one really needs. But we discovered that it is essential to selling in the real world and while there are still businesses that have not yet embraced internet technology, they are now being "lapped" again with Web 2.0 and social media.

- This book is for the business owner who wants to understand Web 2.0 and social media and how it can help their business.

- This book is for the business owner who feels social media is very confusing in it's application due to all of the various "breaking news stories" from social media successes.

- This book is for the business owner who wants to believe that social media is more than just a place their teenagers post videos and music. It's for you if you cannot find an easy solution for a social media marketing system rooted in marketing strategies being taught in MBA programs.

You will learn why social media is so powerful and critical to implement in your business and how it really is much easier to do than you thought, with far less time than you'd think!

While this book is not an academic textbook, it is written for the readers who appreciate that the new technologies we are all hearing so much about these days, are actually rooted in strong business and marketing MBA-level strategy!

I'll reveal the 3-step plan to you here, explain it in the case-study to follow — spotlighting Andy Stubbs — and then summarize with some research and statistics.

So, you may ask: "*Is The P.R.I.S.M. Salvation just another book on social media?*"

My answer is "No. You will learn how to integrate an MBA-level marketing strategy into your business while applying social media as the marketing vehicle in an integrated marketing communication." This is what it's all about:

The P.R.I.S.M. Salvation

- **P**owerful

- **R**elationships

- **I**ntegrating

- **S**ocial

- **M**edia

P.R.I.S.M. Principles:

Here is the 3-step plan:

1. Identify and Magnify Your Competitive Advantage
2. Identify and Clarify Your Target Audience/Ideal Client
3. Deliver Your Integrated Marketing Communication Efficiently and Effectively

What does that REALLY mean?

1. What sets you apart from your competition and makes you AWESOME?

2. Who REALLY is your perfect customer?

3. How do THEY want to be communicated with to learn about the benefits of your company?

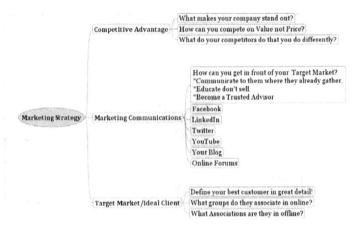

- You will learn why you must weave your marketing message into a "voice" that is conversational and literally attracts customers to you.

- You will learn where to find these tools, and how much they cost (most are free!). The beauty of social media is that the foundational infrastructure is a free model that encourages sharing and interaction. What you will learn in this book is the strategy behind social media systems and how they can work for you — if you decide to purchase additional features to enhance their effectiveness later, that is up to you.

- You will learn how to use these tools, not the basic operational step-by-step instructions, because that can be learned from the social media tools themselves or from a basic Google search. But you need to learn how to use these tools for your specific business to accomplish the goals and objectives you have set out to achieve.

Social media is playing a huge role in the lives of modern professionals and small business owners. Today, the world is getting more and more global while at the same time the use of social media seems to have brought this global power to the local market to attract new customers from their own backyard.

Marketing and branding are two of the most important aspects of a business — small or big — and traditional media seems to run out of steam when it comes to connecting to a large number of customers. This seems apparent when you consider your DVR that allows you to skip right past TV commercials. Or the fast rise of satellite radio where there are no commercials at all, to the fall of so many newspapers because of the drop in advertising revenues and the increase of consumers reading their news online.

The social media fanatics swear that it is lightening fast and will outgrow any other media in terms of efficiency, but while you cannot guarantee the level of social media success, it is a powerful force that cannot be ignored. The craze about social media is not because it helps to take your message to millions within a second, but it helps business owners to get a better insight into the needs, requirements and mindsets of their customers while deepening a more personal relationship with them.

After all, one of the biggest benefits of social media is that it is already happening online. Being able to insert your message into what is already going on makes your message well-received because it is not selling, it is participating and educating your target audience. You are positioned as the trusted advisor. Let me say that again because this is very critical:

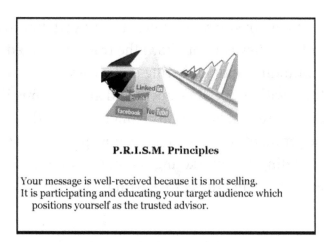

P.R.I.S.M. Principles

Your message is well-received because it is not selling.
It is participating and educating your target audience which
positions yourself as the trusted advisor.

Let's think for a minute about "participating and educating" in the statement above. Does this mean you pop into a forum that is all about the line of business you are in and start typing "buy my product because it's the best!"? Although you may feel tempted to do this because you need sales, you must resist this urge because you immediately become a nuisance.

In fact many social media sites have a Terms of Service that prohibits blatant selling. After all, the true benefit of social networking is just that: networking. By the way, people think just because they show up to a Chamber of Commerce meeting or sign up for an online social networking site that they are "networking." It is not! Take a look at the word: it's "networking." You have to put in some effort!

Small businesses often start out with limited capital and they cannot afford the traditional media for their branding and marketing endeavors. They are very cautious with every dime spent and are watching like a hawk for a return on that investment! But with the introduction of social media it is now possible to carry out branding and marketing campaigns at unbelievably lower costs, many times free, with lightening fast speed.

Do you think that it may just be an "exercise in futility"? Putting forth all that effort, and you'll just be another voice online pining away about your topic?

Consider this, a well-known Internet research expert named Jakob Nielson developed what he called the Community Participation Pyramid which states:

(Nielson, 2006)

1. 90 percent of users in an online forum just read and observe, but don't contribute.

2. 9 percent contribute from time to time, but not on a consistent basis.

3. 1 percent participates a lot and account for the majority of the content.

So what does that tell us?

1. 90 percent of the "power" of a forum is invisible because there are so many "lurkers" not contributing to the conversation — so they will be reading YOUR comments!

2. Be part of the 1 percent. Be influential and trusted.

3. It doesn't take much to be part of that 1 percent, just be consistent and relevant.

P.R.I.S.M. Principles

Consumers truly have the power in today's marketplace because they have the power to turn on and off any content on any topic at any time.

This is perfectly illustrated in a story that happened in 2009 (Silverthorne, 2009)

*When **United Airline** luggage handlers broke **Dave Carroll**'s guitar and a customer service rep bureaucratically weaseled out of fixing the problem, Carroll did what any angry consumer now does: He made a YouTube video.*

Unfortunately for UAL, Carroll, front man for the band Sons of Maxwell, made a good one. And now United has thousands of people writing of similar bad experiences with the airline in posts all over the Web.

To make matters worse, United is responding by fixing the symptom, not the real problem. Says Frances Frei, an expert on customer service at the Harvard Business School:

"United spokespeople now say that they're going to use the video to help the company improve its service, and my prediction is that these efforts will fail. The company's language is tentative. If Carroll's experience illustrates a systematic pattern of failing customers — and the anecdotal evidence suggests that it does — then United's leadership will need to do something much bigger than launch a superficial service initiative."

Take a look at the blog post and watch the videos and imagine how much power one traveler had in this situation!

http://blogs.bnet.com/harvard/?p=3130

So what can we learn from this example? The consumer holds the true power these days. It has always been taught in business school that you should listen to your customer so you can deliver the products and services they want and need. But now it's even more critical because if we don't listen to them, they will start a conversation — good or bad — about our product or service online. This may be on their Facebook page, blog or maybe even a YouTube video that could damage your reputation.

What can be done?

- Learn how to participate in social media networking that is already going on all around you.

- Find where your customers gather.

- Listen to their conversations online.

- Understand their needs.

- Participate and contribute in a helpful way to their questions and comments. Be the solution-provider.

In his ground-breaking book, *Meatball Sundae* (Godin, 2007), Seth Godin says:

"I define Old Marketing as the act of interrupting the masses with ads about average products. Masses of people could be processed quickly and cheaply, and some would respond to your message and become customers. New Marketing leverages scarce attention and creates interactions among communities within similar interests. New Marketing treats every product, service and side effect as a form of media. Marketers do this by telling stories, creating remarkable products, and gaining permission to deliver messages directly to interested people."

So how do we communicate, connect and encourage interaction with groups of our friends? Well, definitely on <u>their</u> terms giving <u>them</u> the chance to decide what <u>they</u> want to view and do. We do this because there is a reason to. There is a public relations firm called Edelman that did a survey (Edelman, 2006) in 2006 that concluded: "By a 3-to-1 margin, people are far more likely to trust average people just like themselves and 67 percent of consumer goods sold are as a result of word of mouth because this is what is trusted more-so than traditional marketing or advertising."

Enter Web 2.0 and Social Media!

For many people the term "Web 2.0" is complicated. They fail truly to understand what it is and how it works. Many so-called experts have tried to give their long, drawn-out technical explanation of this type of website. The problem is experts who use so much jargon and hard-to-understand technical mumbo jumbo that an average person will need a de-coder ring to decipher what these experts are saying!

Web 2.0 websites are user-generated content sites. Visitors to the sites sign up and then start contributing their own content to the site. Facebook is a user-generated Web 2.0 social networking site. Users create their own profiles, add pictures, and upload videos and even music to the site. Social bookmarking sites such as Digg allow users to submit links to stories, videos and websites that they like along with their own review of the pictures, videos and websites in general. Therefore, the majority of the content of these sites are contributions from users just like you.

The way this concept differs from what we know as traditional sites is that the traditional sites are more static. This means that their webmaster generates all the content for the site and shares this content with you, and typically the content hardly ever changes. You, as the visitor, have no say in the content that is on this site nor do you usually have a chance to leave your own opinion of the content.

Author David Meerman Scott wrote the book: *The New Rules of Marketing and PR: How to Use Social Media, Blogs, News Releases, Online Video, and Viral Marketing to Reach Buyers Directly.*

He says that companies should hire employees or marketing consultants to churn out content about their products and services based on solid keyword research and post it on blogs, videos, press releases, articles and various social media sites. This is the new way to promote your company and brand that is the most effective way to reach today's consumer. By doing this, your net is spread so wide that your target audience will find your content and be led to your "online real estate" which could be your blog, social media networking sites etc.

"People are looking to find a community around your service and are looking to have conversation with you about the products they're using." (Brill, 2006)

This is where the significance of social media arises.

Social media, as the name suggests, is a kind of a communication tool. It is an aggregation of online sites that are created by people who are interested in the exchange of views among a wide circle of individuals

The assumption that social networking makes, is that people are inclined to interact and connect with each other. If engineered properly, social media can open up wholly new and potential avenues for the promotion of your business.

One thing to keep in mind is that the social media only assists in promoting your brand, as opposed to creating it. It only acquaints people of your ambitions and goals in life as opposed to being an aggressive sales portal. So before you log on to one of these sites, ensure that you have a brand that has enough meat in it to capture and sustain the attention of your target audience.

This is where you need to deploy the MBA-level marketing strategy that you will learn through the story and application in this book.

Chapter 2
The Story of The P.R.I.S.M. Salvation

A Little Blue Bird Flew Away
With Your Newspaper! A Social Media
Strategy To Win Without Intimidation

As a fresh graduate from college, the question "what's next?" troubled Andy Stubbs. Friends suggested that he move from California and try something new, relatives suggested staying in this small town and try his luck. But no one ever asked what he wanted to do. He had a secret desire to run his own small business, but at this point, he neither had the confidence nor the resources to brave the circumstances and take the risk.

Small businesses in California weren't thriving at that point and he didn't have the guts, support, or motivation to start a small business. He thought he could work on some unique ideas that he was passionate about because he heard the quote once that if you do something you love then you would never "work" a day in your life. He thought that sounded great and even had a few ideas. But then, he didn't know where to start. Ever since he was a kid, Andy absolutely loved tinkering with tools and taking things apart, in fact it seemed like when any appliance in the house broke, it was Andy that could fix it. It just seemed like a natural gift he had and he could spend hours upon hours working on an appliance. It even seemed like when it was done it somehow worked even better than before.

The problem was that he didn't have the needed capital to start his business, but he really felt a burning desire to do something on his own, and he could just see it in his mind. A nice little appliance shop in town where he would fix broken appliances for customers and pick up others that people wanted to throw out to fix and sell for a profit. It would be his dream job since he could remember as a boy missing meals because he just got caught up in his work. In fact, friends from church and neighbors started hearing of his ability and he would fix their appliances, too.

After deciding that starting a business was just too risky, he followed the footsteps of his father and started looking for a nice steady 9 to 5 job. His father had been at the same factory coming up on 30 years and it sure kept a roof over their heads and food on the table all these years. So, of course, when his father put in a good word for him at the factory he was immediately offered a job. Although it was an entry-level job Andy knew that you have to start somewhere.

Now tell me something, how long can someone follow the same schedule day in and day out? Many do just as Andy, and they wind up feeling unfulfilled and missing out on the dreams they had for their life. They could have simply made a plan with small, achievable goals that would move them closer to their ultimate dream. It may take 10 years to get there, but if you don't make any forward progress then in 10 years you are still where you started.

"Keep moving forward" — Lewis Robinson, Walt

Disney Pictures, 2007

Fast forward 16 years later, Andy is married with two children but still there is pretty much no change in his daily routine, the soul and passion was completely missing. He was working like a machine — only to support his family members and help his kids pursue their education.

Sometimes he remembered his dreams and for a split-second it excited him, but then a rush of guilt and regret flooded over him. Andy wished "Oh, how good it would have been if I could have started my own business, things could have been much better. Life would have been a lot different and may be better for my family without me moping around the house all the time." Andy wondered how much actual damage was being done in this situation. Not only was he affected with not taking action on his dream, but it was now affecting his family and people around him.

He hardly made any friends at work and lost the ones that he had due to his growing crankiness. Ann, Andy's wife, Abigail their daughter and Andy Jr., who is his teenage son, had the same mechanical skills his father had and boy did that make Andy feel great! Of course this added to Andy's frustration because it reminded him yet again that it would be great to share his dream of opening a little appliance repair and sales shop with his son. His wife was a constant pillar of support and though she understood her husband's dream, she did not have any professional experience to help him out.

In addition to these three people, another person knew about Andy's dream: Carl Jenkins, the security guard at the factory. Carl was a retired person who worked part-time to keep from getting too bored and was previously employed as a CPA and business owner in a California-based company. He lived down the road from Andy and both of them shared a ride to work a few times a week. These rides allowed Andy to vent his frustrations about work and starting his dream business and since Carl had business experience it was nice to pick up an idea or two. Carl would always tell others, "This man will go a long way one day; he is ambitious but feels scared of taking the plunge. If only I could help him."

One morning, when Andy was busy at his office, Carl called him up, "Hey Andy, I know you aren't happy with your job, your dream is to start your own business, so please make sure you attend today's seminar at the Chamber, I'll be picking you up at 5," then he hung up. He didn't even give Andy the time to say anything. He knew that if he did so, then Andy would definitely make an excuse and once again prevent himself from fulfilling his dreams.

The seminar opened up with an introduction to the Small Business Development Center (SBDC) and its' mission and goal to help small businesses. He found out here that assistance was given to already functioning businesses as well as to prospective small business owners looking to get guidance in getting started. To be more specific, it is referred as one-stop assistance to small businesses. It offers a varied collection of guidance and information in readily accessible branch locations. The program is an important part of training for entrepreneurial development.

What really surprised Andy was the entire section was dedicated to working with people who want to start their own business! "What? Are they for real?" Andy thought.

But as the seminar continued, he learned that there are resources that not only would teach and support him in setting up and running his business, but were provided at no cost!

Andy leaned over to Carl, "There's got to be some catch with all of this right? There's no way that they can do that. Why have I not heard of this before?"

"No, there's no catch, Andy," Carl whispered, "in fact, I used to come downtown and help them out working with people just like you a few years ago and that's why I invited you tonight."

Thrilled with the seminar, Andy looked to Carl and said "Thanks Carl, it helped me a lot. I wasn't aware of the SBDC and the benefits they offer. I wish I had known about them earlier, I could have started my dream project much earlier... anyways thanks again, thanks a lot."

Carl replied, " It's ok, but there's more, you'll be pleased to know that you can schedule a meeting with a SBDC consultant to start working with you and building a plan of action. Andy I always knew that you don't like to be just an employee, you are here to own your own business and I want to help you."

"Wow that's too good; I'll go talk to the SBDC consultant. Can you help me out with his name, Carl?"

"Parker Carswell, the SBDC consultant, will help you out. Just go ahead and discuss your plans with him and don't forget to keep me posted on your progress."

That night Andy came home but with a troubled mind, and not in a bad way. He didn't have his dinner, "I'm not feeling well, you can go ahead and go to sleep, I'll be up late," he told his wife and went for a walk. His mind was buzzing with questions. Questions of opportunity and risks. He woke up early in the morning and decided that he would discuss everything with his wife. After he told Ann all about the seminar and the resources they can provide, she could see the sparkle in his eyes and hear the enthusiasm in his voice. It had been a long time since she had seen that from Andy and it made her feel good. Good for her and proud of him. "I don't really know what step to take, should I go for it or should I just pass on an opportunity? I mean I want to go for it but I'm afraid of the risks" Andy said while having his morning coffee with Ann and the kids.

"Go for it!" "We are with you!" were the immediate replies from his family. They all talked for a while about the various points like: "Should I really do this?" "What if it doesn't work out". But they all were so supportive and encouraged him with their responses. Andy Jr. told him that he secretly had been planning on approaching his dad one day about going into business together and Abigail said that she was taking some bookkeeping classes at school and could help with accounting. Of course Ann said she could do anything that was needed to make the store an attractive and fun place to be. Andy thought about how strange it sounded to have a "fun" appliance repair shop, but then again maybe that was the ticket. Make something so seemingly boring and mundane to be a fun place to be!

"Yes don't think twice, just get started, we're all behind you!"

At this point, Andy felt enthusiasm surge through his body. He was ready to embark on a new journey of his life.

On the way to work he told Carl all about the conversations he had with his family about the seminar. "That's great, Andy, I have a great feeling about this for you."

This was the first time when Andy left home convinced, with new thoughts blooming in his mind. He decided to schedule a meeting with Parker Carswell right away. When he called the SBDC office and was told that

Parker was booked three weeks out! "Yikes," Andy thought. "Well, let me know if he has a cancellation before then, I really need to see him." As he hung up the phone, he felt like a new glimpse of opportunity and success was just starting to peek through the clouds in his life.

At the very first meeting, Andy told Parker all about his journey to this point and while he listened, Parker took notes. Andy hoped these notes were the start to something big in his life. But when Parker started explaining to him the basic foundation of starting a small business, Andy heard something that let a little air out of his sails. Parker first told him not to quit his job right away, instead he advised him to make the transition slowly. He plainly advised him to start off with a part-time business and then commit to it on a full-time basis after it was established. They scheduled another meeting for a couple weeks later and Andy walked out with his list of action steps to work on.

On one hand Andy was a bit discouraged, but then as he thought about it, it made complete sense, why take unnecessary risks? So that night he told Ann all about the meeting and although she sensed his disappointment, she pulled out a sheet of paper and started making plans on how she can help. This started Andy thinking about all the action items Parker gave him and he now felt like he was making progress.

Things at work were worsening; the start of the recession had a negative impact on Andy's workplace as well. His salary was cut by 10 percent. At this point Andy could not afford to quit his present job. At times he felt tempted to quit his job, get rid of his boss's tantrums and start running his own business on a full-time basis. But then the words of Parker kept ringing in his ears.

After being employed in a firm for 16 years, he had gathered a bit of cash, enough to open a business just like the one he and Parker has been talking about over the past month, an appliance sales and repair business. Finally, one day when his day was especially tough, he took his lunch break and went for a walk down Main Street. What he saw almost made him choke on his PB&J sandwich: right there in front of his eyes was a shop with a "going out of business" sign in the window. He knew the owner of the shop, a small office supply and equipment store, and wondered if he was there, even though there was a sign on the door showing they were closed for lunch.

As he was looking through the glass (rearranging

the floor plan in his mind to convert it to his appliance repair shop), the owner walked up. "Hey Andy, what's up?"

"Oh, Ted, I have just got to talk to you, do you have time?"

"Sure, come on in," Ted said wondering what was so urgent.

After Andy laid out his plans that had been formulated over the last few weeks, he walked out of the store with something that made his heart leap and the grin on his face almost hurt: a lease! You see, Ted owned the store building and was retiring after 20 years of running the business. He even told Andy that he would be available to help him convert the store to the layout Andy needed.

When he walked in the door that night, his family heard something they had not heard in many years...whistling.

Andy? Whistling?

"What happened today?" They wondered

It seemed to take only minutes to explain his eventful lunch break to his family, but he was talking so fast he was surprised when Ann told him to take a breath.

"Guys, I think this is the open door we have all been praying and waiting for!"

"I believe if we can work together, we simply cannot lose." So, the four of them joined hands and promised that they would establish one of the most successful businesses in town!

The next day at his meeting with Parker, Andy brought him up to speed and they started immediately on working out his next steps.

Over the next few months in operation, Andy's business showed steady progress. He implemented a couple of traditional ways to promote and advertise his business. For instance he used the newspaper, radio and ads as a medium of promoting his business and reaching out to most of the people in town. This seemed to be all that was needed to bring in some business.

Initially, everything seemed to be running smoothly with people bringing in their broken appliances and the sales of the appliances were also good and he was making a decent profit through his business but things started to slow down a bit. Andy was expecting faster growth and was working extra hours to push his business further. His marketing efforts did bring in some initial results but they were not consistent and he wondered if it was just from the fact that he was new and people were coming in to support him.

But something went wrong; though he always had a knack for fixing things, he focused too much on the tools in his hands and didn't realize his business was dropping off. Andy didn't take this issue too seriously, taking it to be only a rough patch in his business that would soon improve. As we'll start to see, this couldn't be further from the truth. Andy's business started to steadily decline from the opening months.

Now, Andy realized this problem and discussed the issue with his family. Their business would not survive if they fail to change their business strategy. Innovation is the key to success. Ann told him about a few ideas she had been thinking about making flyers to distribute around town and a contest to see who had the worst appliance needing repaired.

They came up with some ideas to take their business to new heights. Ideas such as sponsoring contests, distributing door to door flyers, and marketing phone calls clicked in their mind. They started implementing these tactics into practice, but as they realized, overnight results are not ever possible.

Tired of this situation, the thought crossed Andy's mind to give up the entire venture. He realized that small business was not his cup of tea and it was better to stay with the same old 9 to 5 job. When he mentioned it that night at dinner, he received quite the response: "What are you saying? It's our dream too, we need to turn it into a reality. I agree that we did make some mistakes, we didn't follow Parker's plan exactly like he told us. if we act now, I really believe things will change for the better. Please Dad, let's contact Parker and see if he can help us out of this mess," suggested Andy Jr.

"Parker." The word itself emerged as a ray of hope and Andy decided to contact him right away. He called the SBDC office and said "Parker, I'm in great trouble, none of us took your plan as seriously as we should have and at this moment our business is on the verge of going under. Can you please meet with us?"

The next day, Andy, Ann, Abigail and Andy Jr. all went in to see Parker.

"Come on in guys!" Parker replied with a warm smile". As Andy stepped in, Parker replied, "So, how are you doing? You look really worried."

"Parker, we need your help to find a way out of this mess. I have implemented a couple of ideas but they will take time to work and I just cannot afford that," said Andy wiping droplets of sweat on his forehead.

Parker replied plainly, "I understand Andy, but you have to understand I warned you over and over again to be careful moving ahead in your business because you can't allow yourself to be so pleased that you got out of the 9 to 5 grind that you forget that the business would not run itself. But don't worry, we'll get you all straightened out, I'll guide you.

"First, we need to lay a strong foundation and start off with an MBA-level marketing strategy. Then we'll work together on a social media marketing system." Andy was surprised, he had read about social media but he never thought of using anything like that. After all, fixing appliances isn't too exciting. But at this point, Andy needed all the help he could get and decided not to question anything, so he determined to follow the plan.

Every week Parker and Andy met to map out plans to help bring about a positive change into his business. Parker also helped him with the basics of why you need a marketing plan in the first place. In fact, it's kind of like going on vacation with no idea where you are going and no map. Andy could see that if you don't have a set of plans in place that lead to a final goal objective, you really can't measure where you are or if you are off course. Parker said something that really caught Andy's attention one day and it made him remember something his father used to tell him growing up. "Son, the old saying 'knowledge is power' is a bunch of bunk because merely having the knowledge is not the power. The true power is implementing that knowledge and doing something with it!"

Andy decided that he would heed his Father's advice and not only listen to Parker's plan, but put every step into action. Social media can play a vital role in marketing his products and it can be used to grow the sales figures as well as learn about the needs of customers. They started to discuss how to use the social media marketing strategy to reap slow but long-term benefits. Winning back the lost ground would be easier with this tactic. Parker made another interesting observation that really made Andy think. He said that so many business owners think that social media is just for teenagers to post their pictures and music videos and that made sense to Andy because that's what he thought, too.

"What do I need with the ability to download a ringtone from the latest and greatest one-hit wonder band?" Andy thought. But as Parker explained what social media really is, it dawned on Andy that this was merely just a tool to communicate with people in a way that they are already communicating.

The power of social marketing was now crystal clear to him. Parker told him that over the next few weeks he would be teaching him the major differences between conventional media and new media and how to integrate an MBA-level marketing plan with Web 2.0 to bring about a positive change in his business.

Parker was also able to give Andy suggestions through which he can prevent any competitor from having any major impact on his business. He told Andy that by introducing unique services that are in no way same as the competitors there's no room for competition. Hiring a marketing professional was a part of the long-term strategy as Andy would want to be released from the tactical implementation of the marketing plan. It is true that initially Andy was a bit concerned about the monetary investments involved in hiring a marketing professional, but after understanding that only with focusing on what he does best, and outsourcing the rest, can his business succeed. When he realized that if he tried to train and educate himself in all the areas that he was lacking in his business, that he would be losing money. Parker taught him that he needed to focus as close to 100 percent of his time on what he is best at and this would grow the business. Also, by not having a marketing person on staff keeps the salary and expenses down. Hiring an outside consultant would solve that, and actually save money when the time comes.

Everyone's Favorite Radio Station: "WiiFM" — How To Advertise On It

Parker was sitting in his office and working on his laptop when he heard a knock on the door. "Come in," Parker said, and saw Andy entering the room with a troubled face. "Sit down, Andy, what's up?" Parker asked while still typing on his laptop. "I am fine," Andy answered trying to hide the tides of emotions behind his smiling and ever-courteous face. Taking his eyes off from the laptop, Parker looked straight into Andy's eyes and said, "So what would you like to cover in today's meeting?"

"A competitor moved to town!" Andy said finally.

The word "competitor" came as a shock for Parker; he never imagined that a smaller town like the one they live in can even have competitors who can trouble a business like Andy's. (This was a feeling of déjà vu for Parker — he had attended a seminar during his MBA coursework where a case study matching that of Andy's was analyzed. He did not reveal this to Andy but made a quick note on his laptop to go through the case study later that day.)

"Calm down and stop worrying unnecessarily; we are going to work out a plan and put everything back on track," Parker said while closing down his laptop. "Before we get into the details of what your business is going through and the problems that you have encountered in the last few weeks, I want you to do something — calm down and re-collect your confidence. There is no use dwelling on problems that have not even occurred yet, so it is better that you concentrate on strengthening your present situation that you can control" Parker continued.

For the next hour both Parker and Andy discussed in detail about implementing the marketing plan they started to build.

From the very beginning, after setting up shop, he left the management of the store to Ann and Andy picked up the marketing responsibility. Their marketing plan was drawn to target the middle-aged demographic so they set up a small market survey by calling various customers and asking them about the appliances they currently use and the ones that they are contemplating to buy in the future.

The survey revealed some very impressive responses. There were some extra services and touches in their business that their customers were voicing that were not being provided. These were easy solutions, and Andy wondered why they hadn't dawned on him. "Guess I never asked," Andy thought to himself. So he quickly made a note to implement the small adjustments necessary to be ready to roll these out in the upcoming press releases and social media campaigns they were working on.

"OK, now tell me what you know about this new competitor," Parker continued. Andy described what he knew: NewGen Appliance Corp. was a big brand in the state and as a marketing strategy to penetrate the smaller market, the company created franchises in small towns like his in California. The company was already a known brand and all the franchise had to do was to put in some billboard and newspaper ads to attract the people toward the store. The company also put on some ads on the local radio and that was enough to catch the attention of people.

In the initial stages, Andy did not take much notice to the changes in the market and even down-played the growing popularity of the new company in the market. Over just a few months NewGen ate away Andy's customer base. After a considerable decline in the sales, Andy realized that they had made a big mistake by ignoring the new competitor in the market. Slowly but surely, a downslide started on their sales figures and soon there were hardly any visitors in their store.

No discount offers or gifts would bring back the customers to his store. The new company used the latest technologies to gather information about the customer behavior and market trends. They offered all the high-end products that customers never dreamed were even available.

Marketing appliances never looked to be such a tough job when Andy opened up the business. But with the new entrant in the same niche, he was losing the battle very quickly.

Mistakes That Caused the Downslide

Parker listened to everything that Andy had to say about the events that had occurred in the last six months and had practically changed Andy's life. While discussing, Parker was also taking notes of what steps Andy had taken for implementing his marketing plan.

"So do you know what exactly caused the problems in your business or what exactly caused the dip in your sales figures?" asked Parker. Andy did not have anything to say as this was what he had been trying to find out for a long time. "No," Andy said.

"It is your marketing strategy, or I should say the lack of one, that caused the trouble." Parker replied.

"Marketing is not always directed at prodding your customers into buying your products or services; it is also about knowing the right needs of your customers and catering to their needs in timely manner," Parker continued. "You need to find out about their fears and problems and then solve them. What you tried was to push the products into your customer's home without trying to find out whether they needed them or not. You tried to sell the wrong product and service to the wrong people and it resulted into the customers shifting to a better alternative, i.e. to your competitor."

Parker took out a pen and paper and started to scribble something on it; this looked pretty strange to Andy and he was about to ask what it was when Parker said, "Andy I think we need to redesign your marketing strategy, but first you need to learn something about marketing." Parker further clarified that "it was because you failed in building a relationship with your customers. It was easier for them to move to another brand because your company never left a lasting impression on them."

"But I tried to always ask for genuine feedback from the customers and even provided the best technical support to them. Occasional discounts and gifts were also provided by our company, why did we lose those customers?" Andy asked.

"Andy, marketing is not only about checking the feedback of your customer or trying to attract a customer through discounts and seasonal offers. It is all about getting a hold of the right factors that motivate your customers and knowing their specific needs that you can solve. In fact, did you know that every customer who comes in to your store listens to the same radio station?"

"How can that be?" Andy asked.

"Simple," Parker answered, "it's WiiFM ....which stands for 'What's in it for me'."

"You see, it's like everyone is most interested in what's important to them!"

Unless it is only your brand that plays on the channel, you are not going to build a long term relationship with your customer. Branding is also a vital part of the marketing process and you will have to take this into serious consideration."

Andy never looked at his marketing strategies from this angle and Parker was slowly opening up new perspectives for him. Andy was paying complete attention now as Parker kept explaining.

"We love to tune into our favorite station, too, WiiFM, to find products and services that have something for us. For instance, we try to look at a website and skip the ones that do not look to be of use. In a similar way, we try to find a particular product that is of use to us." While Parker spoke, Andy tried to relate the explanation with the incidents that took place in his business and the reaction of the customers to various situations.

If we look into the broader explanation of marketing and then relate it to WiiFM, we would definitely find out the things that Andy missed out during the past six months.

By applying this new perspective on these points, and focusing on what the customer needs, there is a whole new opportunity to meet those needs.

Parker decided that Andy's main problems were in his marketing plan. Now, he would have to map out a fresh plan and it would require applying this new customer-centric focus to the plan. This time Parker wanted to ensure that Andy understood everything about marketing and would not face any problems. They decided that for the next week Andy is going to come to his office and draw out a detailed marketing plan with Parker. Reassured that his business is now going to make a quick comeback, Andy left Parker's office and went happily home.

Since a marketing plan of any company must be comprised of the proper foundation, it is very important to understand each step. Andy came back the next session with Parker to draw a formidable marketing plan for his company.

Parker started out with a very serious look on his face and said, "marketing plans consist of the strategy to sell a product or service to a particular group of customers and all the marketing efforts are to be directed toward them. Today, we will be looking at how to identify your target market -the people to whom you would be selling your appliances."

"To begin, let's look at how to identify the target market."

"Identifying the target market is really important when selling a product or service. You must present the right product to the right people in the right time of their need or want. This is important because other than "impulse products" like a pack of gum in the grocery checkout line, your products should solve a specific need or eliminate a specific problem. For instance, typically you would not sell basketballs to people 70 to 80 years old. So, we would have to take into account the target market. For instance, you would have to find the age group to which you will market your products and services, too. Find out the people who would be your potential customer, and then you have to segregate these people from the others and specifically target them while creating the marketing plan."

"Every new product or service you add into your business in the future needs a separate strategy that you design. Let's look at an example of a strategy."

"You sell appliances and you need to target a market that is mostly at ease with using the modern electrical appliances. This may exclude certain groups of people. Sure there are always exceptions to the rule but this is the way you need to think."

What you must do is conduct a survey of potential prospects. Once you have asked a large group of people their preferences about their use of household appliances, you will see trends appearing regarding who you will be selling to. This is your target market."

"Since we are considering the WiiFM 'What's in it For Me' angle, we would have to create a marketing plan that would cater to the appliance needs of this target audience. So, the promotional strategies and offers that you launch also have to take into account this fact. What are specific needs that they have? What features and benefits do they want?"

"You need to find out the behaviors of this group so that you understand what their social life is like and how their purchase decisions are influenced. Do they see a new top-of-the-line appliance at their friend's home and ask where they found it? Do they like to shop online for convenience? This is where your competitor scored some big points because they understood that your target market is comprised typically of professionals working in a fast-paced environment and don't want to take extra time with food-prep. Thus, their purchase decisions are also influenced by what they discuss during their lunch break. If it is your brand that they are discussing over a casual chat on the Internet then you are in the money. Your competitor used this aspect to reap huge benefits by using relationship marketing to spread the word about their business."

"You have to reach out to your customers and slowly get them acquainted with your company and its products. You can't push products; you must take it easy and slowly create an impression in their minds. The ultimate goal is solving your customer's problems by introducing various products. And making sure that your products are the best in the market. "Branding is also a very important aspect and your relationship marketing is going to help with this."

"While you are selling your product, there is a need to highlight the core features. You cannot just expect the customers to grab your product when there are so many others in the market. Thus, it is important that you have a USP for your products."

Andy interrupted, "What is a USP"?"

Parker continued, "OK, a USP is a 'Unique Selling Proposition.' It's the classic definition for 'product positioning' I learned in my MBA which basically is how your product is perceived in the mind of the customer. Consider the special characteristics of your products. Are they going to solve any specific problems of the customers? Is there any way to understand how your products are better than the others and why they are supposed to be the best."

"This is what we call the 'competitive advantage' and you would have to make your customers realize that you are the best option available to them. You would have to prove this and words will not be enough. You will have to show your customers that your products are capable of solving all their electrical appliance needs.

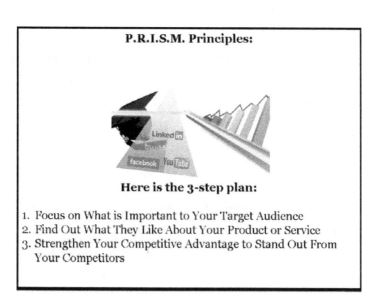

P.R.I.S.M. Principles:

Here is the 3-step plan:

1. Focus on What is Important to Your Target Audience
2. Find Out What They Like About Your Product or Service
3. Strengthen Your Competitive Advantage to Stand Out From Your Competitors

"Sometimes telling them is just not enough. What if you were to hold a weekly 'virtual workshop' online that spotlighted one specific appliance and went over

49

everything from taking it out of the box, to caring for it to last longer, to all the tips and tricks on how to get the most out of it?"

"That sounds really cool," Andy commented." "I'd watch that myself!"

"That's the point," Parker continued, "you want people to feel educated and realize that you are the 'trusted advisor' and source for help. This is also perfect to spread word-of-mouth. And don't feel like you need to build a studio with perfect lighting and perfect video camera and editing. Just buy a flip video camera online and shoot the lessons to post online in a series of workshops. Later once they really catch on you can improve things a bit."

"Here's another angle to take, all your products come with the energy efficient power-saving option. You can stress to your target market that they can save a tremendous amount of money on their power bills every year and that this is taking part in the huge 'green' movement."

All the while Andy was listening to Parker, he realized that his biggest mistake was that he did not even think about his target market. He did recall that his son had once mentioned it, but foolishly he did not pay much attention to it. Research was the most important aspect that he skipped in a hurry to set up his business and this is what created the problem. He never thought that a wrong decision would turn things upside down for his business.

It also hit him that even though social media marketing is the buzz these days, it would be a short-lived vapor if it's not implemented with the solid foundation of a marketing strategy and system.

Now, Parker moved into the most interesting and expensive section of his business. It was the channels of advertisement and the ways he started to spread word about his business. What Andy had done was to use the traditional methods that failed to produce the desired results he needed compared to the latest technologies that were being used. The newspaper ads and radio advertisement slots did not pay off after a period of time. Also, distribution of flyers and brochures did not turn out to be a feasible strategy because it just took too much work.

"You need to use the latest mediums to build

relationship with your customers so that they can access you virtually 24-7. This is provided only by your online presence. This is the most critical piece of marketing for your business today and is how you can establish your brand and credibility in the market. You need to discover where your customers and prospects are gathering online and join in the conversations. Now does this mean to pop up and start selling your products? No, it means that you should find ways to help them understand what you offer in an educational way. This will help you to beat the competition without any trouble." Parker ended the day on this note.

Andy went back to his house and started to write down the things that he had learned from Parker. He had written all the points in details but wanted to have something that he can quickly refer to. He created a list of the important points that were discussed and called the list: "Winds of Change."

- My marketing plan has to be based on structured research that includes every customer's preferences, dislikes, and needs while being segregated on the basis of their characteristics and buying patterns.

- Identifying the target market is one of the primary aims of my marketing plan. After identifying the target market, providing the products or services to the target market also needs to be strategized.

- Competitive advantage needs to be defined and this has to be properly conveyed to customers.

- Advertisements and other marketing tools need to be aligned to reach out to the target audience.

- New methods of marketing should include the basics of relationship marketing wherein emphasis is given on building a long-term relationship with the client.

- "WiiFM" is very important and customers need to be reminded time and again about the things that benefit them.

- Social media tools are to be used to connect to the customers at a personal level while interacting where they already gather.

How to De-Mystify Social Media to Dominate Your Market

The last session proved to be pretty refreshing for Andy as the clouds of doubt began to clear from his mind and he felt a positive energy filling his heart and soul. While coming to Parker's office, Andy felt a surge of renewed vigor and once again he was ready to take the path toward success! Andy learned from Parker that it's very important for an entrepreneur to keep updated on what is available to assist a business owner. He sure was pleased that Carl forced him to go to that first meeting at the Chamber of Commerce. Andy has now come to realize that he banked on the old marketing and advertising media for marketing his products and services. He had been missing out on the opportunities to connect with his customers and prospect base using social media. The best part is that most of these tools are little to no cost!

As Andy entered Parker's room and saw him standing up in front of the table with a pen in his hand and searching for some papers. "Good morning! Are you looking for something?" asked Andy.

"Well, I was looking for a piece of paper that I used for noting a few things. Anyways, let's move to the conference room," Parker said while picking up his laptop. Parker waved him to the left where they entered into a small room that had a big table and projector in the middle.

As soon as Andy sat down in the middle seat Parker started to connect the projector to the laptop and said, "Today, we are going to look at the importance of branding and various mediums through which we can carry out our branding efforts, i.e. the branding tools. Our primary focus of the day's session will be on using social media for branding. Social media for branding is the latest strategy that is going to save your business."

Finishing his speech Parker looked at Andy and gave him a pleasant smile. He then started with his first slide, "Branding is a word that you must learn before planning your marketing strategy. Branding is all about creating a perpetual impression on the mental territory of your customers. This is not an overnight process and would take many months and years for a company to turn into a brand, but it's a process well-worth the effort and really doesn't take any extra time other than considering your Unique Selling Proposition (USP) and how you can provide value to your target audience."

"For the past few months you unconsciously tried to create a brand with your advertisement efforts but it did not sustain for a long period of time as you couldn't hold onto the same position in your customer's mind. Your advertisement efforts were all directed toward attracting the customers who wanted the lowest price and not their actual needs. Remember this, when you compete on price, you will always lose! Certainly there are exceptions to this rule, but for the typical small business you must operate under this rule."

"Branding helps the customer differentiate your products and services from others in the market. You can use social media as a tool to create your brand and also leave impression in your customer's mind of exactly how you can help them. You know, have them tuning in to 'WiiFM'. Actually, it is all about letting your prospects feel that you are the ultimate provider of the product or service."

"All the points of public contact between you and your company are going to serve as the branding point and good branding is all about delivering the message clearly and confirming the credibility of your company, connecting with your target prospects, motivating the buyers and ensuring their loyalty to your business."

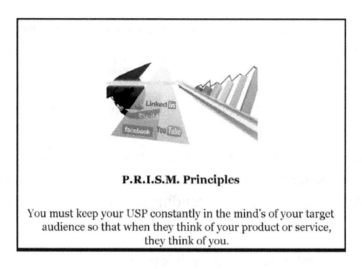

P.R.I.S.M. Principles

You must keep your USP constantly in the mind's of your target
audience so that when they think of your product or service,
they think of you.

"You tried to do a little bit of branding during your
initial days by creating advertisements on the radio —
this was only a part of the entire branding process."

"There are a lot of people who want to retain their
customers but fail to do so with the entry of new
companies in their market. They tend to lose their old
customer base as the new competitors try to use different
marketing techniques to pull in more and more
customers to their business. This in turn creates a
problem for the existing businesses and the cycle
continues with every newcomer in the market. The same
was the problem that you faced when NewGen Appliance
Corp. captured some of the local market. Since your
branding efforts were almost zero it was very easy for

your customers to switch and move over to the new company."

Andy wondered if it would be possible for him to make up the lost ground, so he stopped Parker midway and said, "Well, I know I have flunked the first part of my business endeavor but is it possible to win back the old customers through my branding efforts?"

Parker smiled at Andy's positivity, "It is possible to win back most of the customers with a renewed marketing or branding effort, but things need to be moved on fast before your competitor continues to win the market-share."

"Social marketing is the only branding and marketing tool that can help you to make quick recovery of lost ground. With proper marketing techniques, it is possible to get back to your lost status within a short amount of time and this does not comprise bashing your competitor at any point along the way. In fact, I am thinking of going for a joint venture with your competitor, so that we can tap the market together. What do you say?" said Parker looking at Andy.

This was the strangest proposal that Andy had ever heard and he did not really have any idea about how his company and NewGen Appliance Corp. could really work together to tap the uncovered market. He blankly looked at Parker and saw him smiling. This left him even more confused. "We will come back to the joint venture after I have finished with the social media segment. Better let me deal with one thing at a time," Parker said.

Social Media's Role in Marketing

The latest buzz in the market is all about using social media for branding and reputation management as well as a marketing tool. Though this is a relatively new technique, it is one of the most effective methods available. Parker knew that social media can provide immense benefit to Andy's business and all he would have to do is connect well with his prospects. This is a new concept for Andy, but Parker was quite confident that it would reap huge benefits for the company once it started rolling.

"Social media is the only tool that can allow you to connect to thousands of prospects within a very short period of time. Social media are online platforms like networking websites, blogs, and forums through which you can spread the word about a business, concept, or idea. Actually it's the easiest and most effective way to get 'word-of-mouth advertising'". Parker waited for a while to let his words sink into Andy's mind.

After a few brief seconds, Parker once again began, "It is not possible to judge the needs of your customers easily. Even if you are trying to give personal attention to their problems and doubts, you would not be able to give them the proper attention. In fact, I believe that trying hard the 'offline' way is not effective and if you wish to reap quick results then there is nothing better than going online with your efforts. I call it the 'social media salvation'." If you are interested in building your online brand then you have to integrate all your efforts to make them work in a concentrated harmony. You need to interlink all your social media efforts to create a web in which the customers are going to find you at every corner. Congruency and consistency are two things that you would have to maintain throughout your efforts. Now don't worry, I know this sounds very complicated, but once it is all set up, it is extremely easy to maintain and use, it's just that wherever your customers and prospects are is where you want to be."

"Some of the popular social media tools are the social networking sites like Twitter, Facebook, LinkedIn, blogs and forums."

"You might think that this can also be used to take your revenge out on a competitor, but that is going to do more harm than good to your branding and marketing efforts. On the social media platform everything that you say, write or do is an extension of your company and people visiting your website, blog, Twitter profile, and Facebook page. Your company is going to be judged by your actions. If you become abusive, negative or aggressive, you can cause great harm to your company's image. This is why you also need your own reputation management in place so that your name and brand are being monitored 24-7 and you are alerted when it is discussed online."

"Really? You can do that?" Andy said in amazement.

"That and more, just go to Google and set an alert that emails you every time your business name is mentioned online. I think you're going to like this new world we're moving you into!" Parker replied.

P.R.I.S.M. Principles

1. Create a forum profile for your business on each of the popular social networking platforms that are related to the appliances niche.
2. Connect all the social media platforms together with your blog and website.
3. From one central spot, typically your blog, you create your content and and it will be broadcast to every social media platform you are a member of.
4. The most important tool in your social media marketing: a "Social Media Dashboard".1-Click access to every social media site you are a member of. Everything you need to do in social media marketing is in one spot.

Andy understood everything that Parker was saying but he still was not sure how he could maintain everything on his own. "I am not at all good at working with computers and I don't know much more than checking my email. How can I do this all on my own?"

Parker quickly replied, "I'm going to teach you why everything will work for you because it is based on a solid marketing strategy foundation. Then my 'Social Media Dashboard' will be the only place you need to go for your social media marketing. It will have training and tips, but most important, allow you to communicate with your networks with the least amount of time and effort!"

"Also, I'm here to lay out the strategy for why this

will work, the tactics, or implementation of the strategy, will be a choice you can make. Depending on your level of skill and interest in this fresh new approach to marketing your business through social media, you may want to learn how to set up and use everything. Or you may decide that it's not the 'highest and best use' of your time and energy, and if this is the case I can introduce you to an outside marketing consultant to set it up and run it for you. Don't worry, you don't need to decide now, let's get some more ground-work laid first."

"Once everything is set up, we can focus on more advanced online techniques. I realize this sounds overwhelming in the beginning, but you'll see how easy and effective social media will be for your business."

Soon, Parker and Andy started creating profiles on various networking websites, blogs, and forums. Parker taught Andy that the entire focus of his social media interactions needs to be on helping the people with advice and ideas — not selling. The best way to hint at how he can help is to merely have a customized signature for the forums and social networking sites which appear just below his profile and also every time he carried out activities such as commenting on forum topics and blog postings, this signature would offer something of value like "Request our free video series on DIY appliance repair."

Using a Blog

Blogging was the first social media marketing strategy that Andy and Parker undertook. Parker and Andy met to lay out a solid marketing plan and they already knew that if they can make it big here, then it would be easy to stay in front of their target audience.

Blogging meant that Andy had to brush up his writing skills a bit and Parker helped him with some personal tips in this regard. There are a lot of people who blog on the same niche and Andy had to stand out of the crowd to get noticed. This required choosing an interesting subject to write on and developing his writing style so he could catch visitors' attention.

Parker taught Andy that he must set up a blog and have it hosted rather than getting a free blog service. Free services are typically lacking in the tools and plug-ins to get the SEO that is needed to attract visitors to read your posts.

"This is a very crucial phase and you will have to

take great care in providing posts that are interesting as well as informative. It is better if you start to provide easy tips and other suggestion to the visitors. This will help us to attract more and more visitors," Parker said.

"A blog is a writing space that you can maintain online where you can write anything you want. Your aim is to develop a blog where visitors are encouraged to participate in the content by posting their thoughts on the topic in the comment section as well as returning to seek out more information. You have to build a complete information hub, targeted to your area of expertise so that searches relating to the appliance niche will lead visitors to your blog. I have contacted an SEO expert who explained to me that he will supply you with some keywords to use in your content."

SEO was something completely new to Andy and he learned that it stands for "Search Engine Optimization". Parker got back to his laptop and started to show Andy some slides.

"Search engines like Google and Yahoo have certain programs that track relevant information against entered search keywords. We need to optimize the website for search engine 'bots and spiders' to recognize and give it a higher ranking. An SEO expert is going to optimize your blog and provide it a good ranking and teach you how to use specific keywords in writing your blog posts to attract visitors. This way, when you discuss the competitive advantages of your products and services, people who are searching for those topics will see the link to your posts in their search results."

Inquisitive as always, Andy asked, "How would I determine the competitive advantages of my products or services?"

"Well, that is a very easy job, but remember something: Your blog is going to tell people why they should choose your products or your company above others. There are many people who would love to take a dig at their competitors while informing them about the unique features of their products and services. You must never bash your competitors, instead educate your audience on why you or your company is the best choice for them and let the results and reputation stand on their own."

"You need to build a strategy on some of the unique elements of your products, services and company. This is a very effective way to let people differentiate your company or products from competitors. Let us look at some of elements around which you can build your strategy for competitive advantage."

a) Uniqueness of your product or service-is there something about your product or service that no one else has? What sets it apart?

b) Unbeatable offers-what can you offer that will make your product or service stand out?

c) Attractive packaging-can you package and bundle your product in a unique way? Can you include or bundle extra products and services that bring extra value to the purchase?

d) Mind-boggling guarantee-can you provide such a rock-solid guarantee that the buyer would have to be crazy NOT to buy it?

e) High level of customer service-not just "good" service...above-and-beyond service that makes people run up and down the halls of their office telling people about it!

The importance of creating out a strategy based on competitive advantage works extremely well. Companies that have done so in the past have managed to market their products more effectively and win the confidence of the customers easier and faster than anything else they have tried.

Many people use social media platforms for various purposes, but the thing that Parker was intending to do for Andy was to establish a brand through his blog posts.

Your blog must be exclusively designed to suit your niche so that your posts on the blog are not only interesting to read but also visually appealing. What we must achieve through this blog are:

P.R.I.S.M. Principles

1. Gain popularity in the town of California as well as nearby areas.
2. Build a loyal reader base who need the information you provide.
3. Connect the entire social media identity of your company on the blog.
4. The blog will not only have videos and articles with information on how to repair appliances with ease, but would also have information on all the latest happenings in the world of electrical appliances and new products coming out in the near future.

"Your blog will be the foundation of your marketing efforts. You will get maximum results once you connect your social media networks right to the blog." said Parker.

Slowly, Andy started to draft his blog posts. He had his son proofread them first so to be grammatically correct or flow appropriately.

The blog was not a big hit during the first few weeks but slowly as the number of posts began to increase, the number of visitors also increased. Andy got excited about using his writing abilities to spotlight his products and build his brand. Visitors began to ask Andy questions about appliances and Andy was more than interested in answering each of them.

Parker explained what the nest step would be in their next session. "Since you have already started to post to your blog, we can start with our second phase of work. We will have to create accounts on Facebook, Twitter and LinkedIn. Also, we will create an account on YouTube where you can upload your video tutorials."

"Creating profiles would not take a lot of time but will give wide exposure to your services, products and above all, your company. These efforts will stretch your brand beyond people living in and around your city. Anyone, anywhere, as long as they are online, will begin to recognize your company and your brand," Parker said.

"The people who use social networking sites do so to interact with like minded people and expect to get into casual conversations with the members," Parker continued. "They aren't seeking a conversation with a salesperson. You need to concentrate on getting into discussions that lead to the daily problems people face with their household appliances then people will come back to you for advice. The primary goal is to redirect visitors to your blog and then your online store."

Parker then showed Andy a very important strategy for creating social media profiles. By thinking of the profiles as an abbreviated sales pitch with a personal touch, business owners can connect with their audience immediately. Use the "Unique Selling Proposition" created that spotlights the competitive advantage of the company. Add in a bit about family and hobbies to round out an inviting profile.

Andy decided that his new blog would be all about getting old electrical appliances serviced in minutes. He created a few DIY lessons on his blog that received quite a good response from the people in town as well as people living in nearby towns. Since Andy loved tinkering around with old appliances, it was very easy and natural for him to turn the video camera on and walk the viewers through fixing common problems they may face. At first Andy resisted this idea because it almost seemed like he would be educating people how to NOT come in to see him! But Parker explained that what he would actually be doing is providing so much educational content that they would end up trusting his advice. Plus such a small percentage of people would be skilled enough to complete the repairs on their own and would most likely need his help anyway.

Andy — with specific instructions from Parker—

even registered on several forums geared specifically for technical advice on repairing appliances where he solved the electrical appliance related problems of many people and offered instant and free solutions to most of the visitors. He even posted some YouTube videos on his blog about repairing the old electrical appliances for general households. He then proceeded to create a step-by-step instruction guide where any average person can get their electrical appliances repaired on their own. This proved to be such a fun and well-received project that his base of loyal viewers started to grow very fast. He found that reading emails from people who saw his tips was really exciting, and he was just beginning to see his store traffic increase as well.

His blog was named "Appliance Man" and was mainly targeted at the people who lived in and around town. This was a process and took many weeks for the comments to start arriving on his blogs and forum postings. At times he even started new threads on the forums and started discussion on the new electrical appliances that were arriving in the market with tips and tricks on using them. This was not all. Andy created a website where people were able to directly purchase his company's products from the comfort of their own homes, and as a bonus they would receive the "Appliance Man DVD Tutorial" which was a compilation of his videos from the blog. He would group them together by brand so that someone who bought a specific appliance would receive the DVD showing them how to care for it to maintain the quality and the videos on how to perform the most frequently occurring repairs in the future.

He started noticing that people were raving about the DVD tutorials and sales began to increase because of this one little idea. In one of the meetings with Parker Andy mentioned this, almost in passing as he was leaving from their meeting.

"Wait a minute," Parker stopped Andy. "You're telling me that you've seen increased sales of appliances through your website because you got the word out on your social media networks about your video tutorials that come with the purchase? So, you have discovered that social media is not as hard as it initially seemed."

"That's right," Andy replied thinking nothing of it other than a nice boost in sales.

What Parker was about to teach him the next week would add another stream of revenues to his business, and his social media networking would be just the ticket to launch the idea.

"Come on in Andy," Parker motioned for him to sit down. "Thanks for coming in today, I know it is not our scheduled day but this can't wait!"

Wondering what was up, Andy said, "Parker is something wrong?"

"Oh no, just the opposite, I just put together a new addition to your marketing plan that I really think you'll like!"

Andy relaxed a little and settled in for what would turn out to be quite the exciting meeting. Parker explained that when Andy mentioned how excited he was about the increased sales by adding in the tutorial DVD that he was focusing on one positive thing, but missing out on a new opportunity. If this DVD was the motivating factor for many sales, then that should become a stand-alone product offering to create a new revenue stream and also serve as a lead-in to buying appliances from Andy's store.

By creating an outline for a series of tutorials on all the top questions customers typically have before buying, and the tips and tricks to using the appliance to the fullest given all the technology on most devices that never get used, customers and prospects will buy this as a way to educate themselves on the model they are interested in. The possibilities are almost limitless given the vast amounts of products and models on the market, and choosing the top-sellers will attract the best attention.

"But wait, Parker," Andy interrupted, "What if all these sales come in for these DVD's and now we have to spend so much time packaging up the orders that it takes away from our business ... I don't think I can afford to do that."

"Great point," Parker replied. "But I've got that handled. All you need to do is to produce the videos and get them to a fulfillment company that will duplicate and package each order and ship it to the customer for you! For example, Kunaki and Vervante are two companies that do this hands-free for you and all you do is price your DVD enough that it covers their fulfillment cost and then leaves the profit you need to retain."

"And if you want to do another easy step and reach a different audience and earn higher profit margin, you also offer the DVD series as an online product where they are paid for and viewed right on your blog. This way there is no fulfillment costs, other than some extra bandwidth on your server which is too small to worry about, and this attracts the crowd that doesn't want to wait for a product in the mail and wants to view it immediately."

As Parker continued discussing the plan, it was also revealed to Andy that the DVDs are also a wonderful way to get more prospects to become customers because once the order is placed and they receive their product, whether it is a physical product or immediate download, their email address is entered in the database as a customer. Now, when new videos are ready, they are notified of the free ones to watch and the full-length ones to buy. But most importantly, as his website runs a special on an appliance or the store has an event, they can be instantly notified. This is a very powerful way to communicate to your target audience and earn "back-end" profits, or revenues after the sale.

Parker added one more critical piece of advice: "Andy, the fortune is in the follow-up. You absolutely must use your social media networking to generate interest in your business and have a way to stay in touch with these people to remind them you are still there with great offers. The best way to do this is an automated email delivery service where the free introductory video tutorials you offer are delivered over the course of a week spaced every couple of days. At the bottom of each email is a 'P.S.' to offer a special on appliances in the store or on your website. And the best part is that it works for you 24-7 on autopilot. You just set up the initial series of email messages and tell the system when to deliver them and you're done, of course as this list builds, you can send out broadcast announcements to them about your coupons and special events etc."

"I recommend an inexpensive and easy service at www.emailfollowupservice.com"

"So, how do I tie this in to the social media strategy," Andy asked, obviously excited about these new streams of possibility.

"That's the easy part." Parker replied. "You know how you have your profiles set up on all the social media networks that you are interacting with? Now all you do is start asking your audience what tutorials and brand and models they would like to get help on. This is the fastest and most effective way to create a product, just ask your audience! You can set up a simple online survey that people can complete and it notifies you of their answers, then you can use this feedback to create and adjust your product offerings."

Parker continued to explain how many of the social networking services, like Facebook, have a section where you can paste a simple code on your page, which is generated by the email follow-up service, so that it offers the video series and collects the visitor's email address to deliver the follow-up's. This is an extremely powerful and often overlooked opportunity with social media marketing. Yes, you are there to give and educate, but also if you can offer a simple way to benefit the target audience and deliver it in an automated system to remind them of other offers and discounts you have, then you are truly capitalizing on your social media marketing.

The Facebook Experience

The Facebook experience for Andy was too good to be true. After creating a profile he started to search for the people who lived in and around his town and to his amazement, he found a lot of people within his target market. Andy used an advanced search and imported his personal email list to connect with people who belonged to the 28 to 40 age group and had a stable income. Ultimately, Andy created a list of 471 people and each received an invitation to become a fan of his company page.

Most of the people acknowledged Andy's request and he immediately began communicating with them through answering questions and starting discussions on various topics. He began a conversation with people about rising electricity bills and how using the correct electrical appliances are key to cutting down on costs. He started to connect with various people and asked them for suggestions — engaging in the true form of "social networking." This discussion proved to be the turning point in Andy's entire Facebook-based marketing endeavor. He started to tell people about the video tutorials he made and products that his company sold.

Comments on his Facebook account also started to flow in and Andy began to see what all the "Facebook fuss" was all about. He found it to be pretty fun! He started posting the same video tutorials he made for his blog and started seeing wonderful comments and responses. Then he added a small ad box generated from the email follow-up service on his page to offer his free video series. This collected an email list of those interested in his tutorial videos which would automatically send them updates on his blog and special coupons and offers. Of course, his profile included the blog's web address which started to register an increasing number of visitors in his Google Analytics account. This free tool gives insights into website traffic and marketing effectiveness. It was a simple process to paste a code on his blog so that Google could track where each visitor came from and how long they stayed on his blog and what pages they viewed. Andy found it amazing to log in and see the spike in traffic from Facebook alone. This was an exciting experience for him because he knew that in time, many of the visitors to his Facebook and blog would become customers of his company.

P.R.I.S.M. Principles

1. Create an engaging profile using your USP and personal flair.
2. Find potential contacts to connect with from sources you already have.
3. Focus on QUALITY of the network...not the QUANTITY. It's better to have 50 connections that interact with you than 5,000 just to say you have that many!

No longer is Facebook just a fun social spot for teens, it is now one of the strongest mediums for business owners to connect with any age group. In February 2009, statistics showed that the fastest growing demographic group of users in Facebook was females 55 years old and older. (Smith, 2009)

80

As the weeks continued, Andy was busy with his online management of social media networking (and having fun with it as well!), in fact, Andy Jr. began to maintain the website blog that his father had set up. He took care of uploading the pictures of new products and even updated their descriptions or price on the website to stimulate sales and helped shoot and upload the video tutorials. This became such a hit with their audience that they began to learn how to edit the videos with some nice effects that made them even more fun to watch.

Andy Jr. even set up a "YouTube Branded Channel" with their store logo and details as a background so it was personalized. This channel had all of their introductory training videos loaded in there for people to view and of course links to their social media sites and a way to order their DVD series. Over time, it also became a wonderful way for Andy and Andy Jr. to bond and spend quality time together.

P.R.I.S.M. Principles

1.Create a Product from your current services to provide free as an introduction
2.Introduce the product on your social media platforms and create your "YouTube branded channel" to host all your videos.
3.Have an automated follow-up system to stay in touch with the list you are creating

The social media campaigns started to increase the flow of the traffic to Andy's blog, as well as more and more customers trickling into the store. There were regular visitors to the store who wanted to ask about new products or get their old appliances repaired, and they always were commenting on how much they liked his video tutorials.

In fact, one of the early comments Parker made was now showing some promise. When NewGen moved to town, Andy thought they would put him under, but with a unique twist of business strategy Andy has turned it to an opportunity.

Common Ground With Your Competitor.

One day Andy had just about had enough hearing all about the competition, so he marched right over to their store and asked to talk to the owner. At first Andy was pretty nervous because he was afraid he would say something he would regret later, but as he introduced himself, he just felt a sense of camaraderie for some reason. As they spoke together about business, Andy realized that he was finally learning the true meaning of the marketing strategies that Parker has been teaching him. This is because he realized what "radio station" this owner was listening to and Andy listened for what his true pain and need was. He learned that they actually sell totally different appliances to completely different target markets. This was a revelation that got Andy excited, not only for the opportunity to work together, but also that he thought of the idea right on the spot! Andy made an offer that the other owner absolutely loved.

"So, if I hear you correctly," Andy started, "Your customers and my customers are totally different and we sell very few similar items, it's almost like we're not even competitors! And you just told me how frustrated you and your customers are when the appliances come in for repairs and you cannot fix them and have to send them off to the manufacturer. How great would it be if I did all of those repairs for your customers in my shop? Then you're customers are happy and you are relieved of that burden! In fact, you can even take my invoice and add in a small mark-up to create a new stream of revenue for your store." Andy commented.

This idea was immediately received with open arms and there almost seemed to be an enormous burden visibly lifted off of the owner. As they continued to talk, Andy added another aspect to his offer.

"I would suspect that there are a few of the brands you sell that are similar enough in how they work that I could easily create a series of video tutorials for you to sell on your website and we can split the revenues. This way you are meeting the needs of your customers, as well as receiving increased revenues from a product you do not need to create or sell!"

Of course, this proposal was immediately agreed upon and as Andy left the store with a plan in place, as well as a few work orders for repairs, he wondered to himself whether those thoughts and ideas would have come to him so naturally if he hadn't met Parker Carswell at the SBDC. He realized what great strides he has been making!

"Do you realize the magnitude of the deal you just struck?" Parker exclaimed as Andy called him from his cell on the way back to the shop. "Not only did you set up a joint venture for repairs and your DVD tutorial series, but you have successfully struck a deal that will keep your shop in front of your competitor's customers. Now, I realize you are not looking for ways to put them out of business, but you told me that they sell a very limited line of products that are very different to yours, so there's no worry that he will lose those sales to you, right?"

"That's right," Andy agreed.

Parker continued, "But what you don't realize is that there is an entire series of add-on products that every single one of those customers don't even know that they need ... and you sell them in your store and on your website!"

"And here's another thing, you know how at a restaurant you get one of those pagers to tell you when your table is ready? Why don't you do the same thing — but with social media. Every customer that drops off their appliance for repair, you can tell them to log into their Facebook account right on the store laptop and follow your profile to receive text updates. Then when their appliance is done, you simply update your wall with a message that they can come back in for a pickup. The beauty of this is that not only are you implementing social media, but they become new social media contacts for you, and then every single new repair order is a marketing 'event' because all of your friends and contacts see how fast you work."

"Plus," Andy chimed in with an idea of his own, "just like they logged on when bringing their appliance in, we can ask them to comment on our Facebook wall on their experience and that will give us even more credibility."

Parker just nodded and smiled, knowing that Andy was seeing the true power of social media networking and marketing.

Over the next few days Andy put together a simple plan to present to his new business alliance. This plan outlined all of the ways that they can promote their alliance to each other's customers, and even a big open house and cook-out to announce their new direction. What they discovered is that separately they were competitors, but together they were strategic alliance partners. This is powerful.

Quickly, Andy's store began to get busier and he started to get overwhelmed with all of the tasks of running his business but would always feel refreshed when he read the messages from people in town when they wrote positive comments about his business on his blog or Facebook page. This helped him to slowly get back on track. He also loved "making money while he slept" because a few days a week he would see notifications of DVD sales made that came in overnight! Boy, what a different way of doing business this was.

After a few weeks, Parker called Andy in and said that it is time that they make their next big move which would establish Andy's business with even more powerful joint ventures. Parker went right to the room that Andy was using as his makeshift office and even before settling down he chirped, "Andy, it is time for the big move and you need to do this real carefully. Once you succeed in this, you are going to enter into a whole new realm of business." The excitement in Parker's voice was palpable and even Andy could feel his heart pounding. All these days he has worked day and night to just grab the attention of his customers and there was no way he was going to hear the word 'failure'.

Parker continued with the same excitement, "Since you are already aware that the people living in and around this town know about your services, now you can infuse more credibility and faith into your products. That can be done only if you get to position your products as quality and credible products. This will require a laser-focused campaign where you are going to get endorsed from experts which will help to project your products as the best in the market."

"We need to get your services endorsed through industry experts. This means you have to get in touch with the people who are already holding a credible position in the appliance business. It's not easy to win the confidence of experts, so from now on, start focusing your messages and comments toward catching the attention of these people."

So, they started to search Twitter and Facebook to find experts in the appliance field. The first day did not get them great results though they had started to follow some of the industry experts. Later as the days passed, more and more experts were added to Andy's list and soon the list included industry leaders in the appliance business.

During the initial stages, the communication was generally one sided as none of the experts answered or tweeted replies to what Andy said. This was a little disheartening but one sudden incident changed the way things were moving.

One fine morning, Andy woke up to a call from Parker, "Wake up! This is the big day we were waiting for. Log on to your Facebook account and see. Give me a call back after logging in."

Andy jumped out of his bed and switched on the laptop to log on but did not see any messages for him nor did he find anything of his interest except an inquiry about a recent video tutorial Andy posted on his wall, from one of the experts. He picked up his cell and called Parker who picked up the phone before the first ring completed.

"Did you see that?" blurted Parker.

"Well there is nothing that would interest me except that I just answered one of the comments posted by Brian McMillan," answered Andy.

"You really did that? I mean you knew the solution to the problem with the electric coil?" said Parker with a tone of disbelief in voice.

"Yea, I did. You know Parker, I can repair better than I can sell." boasted Andy.

"Do you realize that you may have just made one of the most important connections in your social media networking so far?"

"How is that possible?" asked Andy. He was quite surprised at why Parker was giving so much importance to a solved query. "Parker, I can't get what you are trying to say. Just tell me what exactly you are so excited about."

"Do you know whose question you just answered?"

"Not exactly, he seems to head some company named Future Technologies Inc."

"OK I am coming in an hour to my office. Meet me there and I will explain why I am so excited." Parker said.

Andy was the first to arrive at the SBDC office and Parker arrived a little late. Parker was beaming like a child and was even whistling when he entered the room and greeted Andy in tone that Andy had never heard from Parker before.

"Good Morning! You asked why I am so excited and the reason is that we have finally broken through to the elite. Brian is not only the head of Future Technologies Inc., but he is also the man who can be your stepping stone to success because his company is breaking the mold of traditional household appliances. When you can learn all there is to learn about his line and create one of your tutorial series for him, you can not only help him launch his line, but go along for the ride with increased DVD sale revenues."

"Just imagine when Brian finds out that you have answered one of his problems. He is going to listen carefully to everything that you have to say about electrical appliance repair," said Parker in one breath.

"Another great point is that his comments and discussions with us will be treated more seriously by members of his sphere of influence and we'll be even more popular among these industry leaders. So, all of the people that look to him for advice, seeing his interaction with you, will transfer that trust to you"

Andy started to understand what Parker was saying. Parker said, "Your interactions with Brian will even help you to tap into the market that has been very difficult to connect with — an opportunity that will help you to create strategic alliances."

"OK, I think you have a point. So how should the level of discussion go with Brian?" Andy asked.

"During the initial stages it is better to keep things light but once you have created a certain comfort level with Brian, you can start to move on to more serious business. Brian is out there with a purpose and he would also like to seek professional alliances with people like you. Don't forget he too wants to tap your market."

This was a confident reply from Parker. This is one strategy that Andy was not aware of, but Parker knew from the very beginning. He was waiting for the right time and Brian's interaction with Andy paved the way for this bigger strategy.

"There is no reason to go overboard with your discussions. I suggest you initially avoid talking about business. But if you receive any such signals from his conversations, then make sure you answer professionally and mention your interest to work with him."

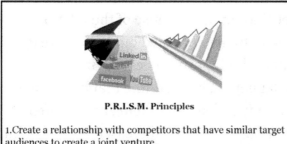

P.R.I.S.M. Principles

1.Create a relationship with competitors that have similar target audiences to create a joint venture.
2.Create a relationship with industry experts and thought-leaders in your field so their audience is exposed to you on the social media platforms
3.Create a product you can offer to the strategic alliance partner so they can introduce it to their audience and you both can benefit.

For the next few days it was only Andy and his laptop. Ann was never really bothered about Andy bringing business home, but recently she noted that he was getting irritated about smaller things. Andy was maintaining too many things single-handedly and it was taking a toll on his family and normal social life. Lately he didn't attended parties or spend much time with his wife. All this troubled Ann to no end — this was not the man she married and this is the reason why he was feeling even worse. She just hoped that things at work would even out soon.

The joint venture with Brian was a great strategy

that brought amazing results. More and more people were recognizing Andy's company and now, customers were not only were restricted to California, but also spread over the country because of the relationship with Brian's firm. Actually, it turned out to be a great opportunity for both parties because Brian was so focused on launching his new line that he had never considered Andy's idea. Now, being able to offer DVD tutorials, not only was there increased revenues, but also there was a dramatic increase in awareness in Brian's product line.

Andy's popularity continued to grow on the different social networking platforms. As a result, the number of visitors to Andy's blog increased tenfold.

The huge popularity of his "Appliance Man" blog was because Andy provided essential tips related to the best-use and maintenance of household electrical appliances.

On one busy morning he received a call from Parker. "Andy, things are moving pretty fast and there is one thing that you need to add to your campaign. You need to ask your customers and readers to post comments and ideas on Facebook and your blog. This would make things more interesting and interactive."

"Well that would definitely make things more interesting," Andy said, "but won't we become vulnerable to the people who want to ruin the company's image? I mean, any mischievous person can post negative comments and create a sense of distrust among the other visitors."

"No, don't worry, that won't happen, your blog is set up with a CMS (content management system) which provides you with the ability to approve each one before they are posted. For every comment you receive on your blog posts, you will be able to generate some good SEO (Search Engine Optimization) because Google and the other search engines see activity and that is good for your traffic. So rather than having a static website where nothing ever changes, you will have the benefit of frequent blog posts. And now with each comment and your reply, you receive extra search engine benefit. This is so vital because in order to be seen you must improve, or optimize, your website based on what the search engines look for. This includes adding keywords in the right spot and a description in the code so that it shows up in Google properly." assured Parker.

"OK, so I am going to be in control of the comments posted on my blogs, but what about comments on Facebook?"

"The comments on Facebook can be easily controlled as you have the option of deleting them, but if comments against your company are made on other online locations that you cannot control, then it cannot be removed."

"This is why you should have social media monitoring done for your company as a form of 'reputation management' so that if this ever happens, you can quickly go into action to get the comment pushed down so far in the rankings that it does not matter."

In the next full length session that Parker and Andy had, Andy received insight into commenting and the detailed method of filtering comments on his blog and other social media platforms.

"Comments on the blogs and forums are going to make your company the talking point on all the platforms and give you maximum exposure. Specific comments on your blog will really help in pulling in more and more traffic to the site. You have a valid reason to ask others to comment on your blogs," said Parker.

"OK, I understand that traffic is very important, but what I am worried about is the security of my blog and won't commenting attract unwanted customers?"

"The effect of negative comments can be easily controlled on your blog, but as far as the security is concerned, you would have to hire a technical person to make sure there are specific plug-ins installed to make it more secure."

"All of this is a form of Word-of-mouth marketing. That is exactly what we are trying to do. We are trying to provide maximum exposure to you, your company, its services, and products."

Now, Parker posed the question of the day: "Do you have any reason to think that blog commenting or the forum commenting is not needed?"

"No, I am pretty clear about the idea and will start putting this in action right away!"

Social media and marketing go hand in hand

because of one reason: Marketing is all about grabbing attention and social media ensures that a brand or a person gets a perpetual presence in the virtual world.

P.R.I.S.M. Principles

1.Make your blog and social media interactions friendly and open to discussion.
2.This creates conversations that lead to new business
3.This improves search engine rankings due to the new content from each comment

Promotion of a brand becomes really easy with the help of social media tools. A company or an individual can easily use Facebook, Twitter, LinkedIn, YouTube and others to spread the word about their brand.

Some of the biggest advantages of social media networking are:

98

a) It is faster: There are a lot of people who are engaged in social networking and can help to spread the word about a business, which in turn helps to brand and market the company and their products. But this is not something that you can expect with typical conventional marketing methods. The lightning-fast effect of social media is the No. 1 thing that has made it so attractive.

b) People love to stay in touch: Most people who take part in social media like Facebook or Twitter love to stay in touch with others who share a similar mindset. So, this can be used by any marketing plan to achieve their marketing results quite fast.

c) Connect with a greater number of people: A large number of people can connect with single thread. With social media you can grab the attention of a large number of people and certain industry professionals.

d) Social media helps to acquire easy and valuable information. You can meet many people and acquire information about a particular niche. For instance, Andy deals with the appliance niche and he could get a good amount of business-related information by getting into discussions with people like Brian who is a joint-venture strategic alliance.

e) Affordability: Social media marketing campaigns are very cost effective as you don't waste money with regular ad campaigns. Spreading the word about your company, products or services online is the solution.

f) Social media marketing helps to gain traffic: If a company wants visitors to be redirected toward their main website, then it can be easily done through the use of social media.

g) Only quality traffic gets redirected: The best thing about social media marketing is that traffic that is driven to the blog or the official website is all quality traffic. Since social media tools target only the target market, there is no chance of people with interests in other niches turning to the website.

h) Search engine friendly: Blogs are highly search engine friendly. To achieve positive SEO, add relevant keywords to your posts. Search engines like Google and Yahoo will give it a higher indexing, especially when there are comments to your blog posts.

In the previous sections, we got to see how Parker used social media platforms for branding and marketing Andy's company. This is definitely one of the most important aspects of new-media marketing. Now, we'll look at the marketing plan in alignment with the social media.

P.R.I.S.M. Principles

1.Social Media and a solid marketing plan are to be aligned together for best results.

2.Social media can give enormous exposure to a company.

3.Twitter Facebook, LinkedIn, blogs, forums and other social media tools help spread the word about your company faster than any other marketing tool available.

4.Social media gives an opportunity to interact more freely with your customer base and provides a good insight into the customer's buying trends and behavior.

5.This marketing plan is the cheapest yet the most effective way to increase business.

Creating a Tribe of Raving Fan Followers

Creating a network of good social media connections was not an easy task for Andy during the initial stages.

Since one of the most critical concepts to understand in social media networking is "quality over quantity." This means that you should never focus on the amount of friends and followers you have on any given social media network, it does not matter if you have five or 5,000. You MUST create a tribe of raving fan followers. This means that your followers should be responsive and interact with each other. They should bring up good topics of conversation and be helpful to each other. This cannot be done if your group is so large that most of them do not know who you are. It is very tempting to aim for big numbers as a bragging point, but you must resist the urge and focus on a good, quality network.

Regarding the term "networking," as in "social media networking," remember that the term is "net-WORKING." It's not "net-join-a-group-and-sell-sell-sell".

Remember:

- You must work at relationships.

- You must give first.

- You must create a warm, friendly environment that encourages interaction.

There are plenty tools that could be used for social media marketing, but Parker picked up the ones that prove to have the highest popularity and at simultaneously provide the necessary exposure to the company, its products and services.

The LinkedIn Network

LinkedIn is a great tool for networking online and connecting with people you work with now or have worked with in the past. It also allows you to create new business relationships. LinkedIn was an easy addition to social media networking because the basic concept was the same: connect and communicate by contributing to and educating his audience. LinkedIn attracted a completely different type of audience which tends to be more business oriented executives.

The biggest difference between Facebook and LinkedIn is the area of introductions. Unique to the LinkedIn culture is the ability to see who your network knows and who can make an introduction to a contact you'd like to meet.

Just like with any social network, it's important that you take a little time and get to know the culture and this is often done by observing a bit. Use the time to build your profile and network of current friends so you can see examples firsthand of how people connect and contribute. Then you can begin to contribute and seek out connections with proven leaders in the network. Andy read demographics that really opened his eyes. Recent

LinkedIn statistics show the following data:

- Average Age: 41

- Male: 64 percent

- Household Income: $100K+ = 53 percent

- Own Smart Phone or PDA: 34 percent

- College Grad/Post Grad: 80.1 percent

- Business Decision Market: 49 percent

- Portfolio Value of $250k+ = 24 percent

- Job Titles:

    o C-Level Executives: 7.8 percent

    o Executive Vice President/
      Senior Vice President: 6.5 percent

- o Senior. Management: 16 percent

- o Middle Management: 18 percent

This type of audience motivated Andy because he knew that their time was very valuable and the last thing they wanted to do on a Saturday morning was to worry about broken appliances. Also, he felt that they would be very open to saving money and time with his video tutorial lessons. What began to happen using this site is that the "tone" of his communications began to become more formal, and he liked that for a change. Not that the casual feel on Facebook was bad, just that LinkedIn was a nice fit for connecting with strategic alliances.

There are many ways to used LinkedIn and a great resource is found at: http://www.linkedintelligence.com/smart-ways-to-use-linkedin

This resource is intended for people who:

- Are new to LinkedIn and need help learning how to promote their business

- Have been using LinkedIn awhile but feel like they haven't really accomplished anything with it

- Are trying to persuade their friends to join LinkedIn and want to communicate the value proposition

- Think there's no real value in LinkedIn

P.R.I.S.M. Principles

1. Form a solid network of your connections remembering quality over quantity.
2. Stay active and maintain a "give to get" attitude.
3. Look for introductions you can make to people in your network and others you'd like to be introduced too.

Mastering Twitter

What is Twitter? Twitter is taking the internet by storm and there are around 10,000 new users per day signing up to participate in this internet revolution.

Twitter is best described as a micro-blogging platform. You are limited to 140 characters each time you write an update, which initially, may seem small. However, as you become more experienced, it's just amazing what you can fit into 140 characters.

That said, Twitter is much, much more than that. It is one huge global chat room, but can also be as small as your community. Everything depends on how many people you follow on Twitter. If it's in the thousands, then your "Tweet stream" will run fast and furious with everything that's coming in. If you are only following a few hundred, or even less, then things are much easier to keep up with.

There is a very disturbing trend going on with Twitter that you need to keep in mind. This is the mind-set that Twitter is a type of "money-machine" to pitch your products and links and any get-rich online scheme to followers. You will see many, many "build your Twitter followers to 10,000 or more in 90 days and earn money while doing it" tweets. Resist the urge to build a large following at the expense of building a quality following. It is far better to have 500 followers who listen and respond to your tweets, than 5,000 who don't! Period.

Twitter came easy to Andy. He created a profile and the number of followers grew quickly as word spread on Andy's blog, Facebook and LinkedIn accounts. He contributed to Twitter simultaneously with the other social media because he knew that people monitor multiple social media accounts and he didn't want to miss out on connecting with potential customers.

Twitter was a relatively easy task, but Andy found it difficult to concentrate on all accounts at the same time. Facebook and LinkedIn consumed most the time he scheduled for social media marketing. On top of that he was busy writing his blog. The work pressure proved to be too much. He wanted to find a way to manage all his social media and didn't know anyone other than Parker who could help.

Andy brought his concerns to Parker who promptly replied: "It is time to go the automation way. We'll use Twitter tools available online to automate the process", Parker said.

Andy heard the term "Twitter tools" for the first time and asked, "How are these Twitter tools going to help in reducing my work load?"

"Tweeting on a regular basis can be a problem especially if you are handling other social networking sites. You can automate you tweets and reduce the pressure of work. This can be done by scheduling your tweets on a particular day and date using many twitter platforms available."

Twitter Tools

The biggest problem with the standard Twitter web application is that you need to keep an eagle-eye on their replies and direct messages as you only see the main Tweet stream on your homepage. The stream is also limited in that it only displays about the last 20 tweets, so to see older ones, you have to keep going back pages. So what to do?

Easy, download Tweetdeck from www.tweetdeck.com. The first thing you will likely need to change is the settings as the default is white text on a black screen which makes it hard to read.

Tweetdeck is brilliant because it displays the Tweetstream, your replies and your direct messages all on the one screen. The message columns allow for 500 tweets as a default, so scrolling down allows you to go back a fair way or search for tweets you may want to refer back to.

The screen has a continuous right-hand scroll, so you can set up different groups and with tweets appearing in that column. You might have a group for friends and another for business contacts, for instance. That way you don't miss important tweets from people who are more important to you than others. At the time of publishing, Tweetdeck is probably the most widely used application for Twitter and is highly recommend by social media experts.

Twellow, www.twellow.com, is another great way of finding people to interact with. People here are categorized into all different areas and you can search for those with similar interests to your own.

The main page shows all the categories, which then have sub-categories. Click on a category and the list of people in that area is displayed. You don't have to be registered with Twellow to be displayed. At the time of publishing there were over 17 million profiles on the sites — so you will have plenty to choose from.

Register yourself and set up a profile so others can find you, too. When you click on a category, Twellow displays a list of people in that category ordered by the number of followers they have. If you are already logged into Twitter, you will be able to follow people directly from the screens where their profiles are displayed.

Andy liked the usefulness of these Twitter tools and said with their help he would be able to concentrate more on his blog writing and video projects.

Andy learned that with the right tools he could intertwine each of his social media networking sites. As the days passed, Andy learned how to set up the Twitter account so that it ran via automated process. One of the unique ways of providing content, in addition to having his blog posts feed into his Twitter stream, was to find industry-relevant topics online. Then, by finding their RSS feed address on the site, he set it up on a tool, www.TwitterFeed.com, where all of the updates on that site feed right into his Twitter feed!

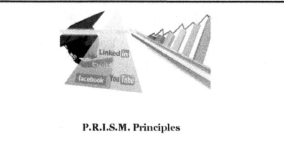

P.R.I.S.M. Principles

1. Create an engaging profile using your USP and include the URL to your blog.
2. Follow and communicate with people you want to connect with.
3. Use Twitter tools to locate specific people talking about specific topics in specific geographic areas.

YouTube: So you don't look like a movie star? Video Marketing will still work for you

One day Andy heard the concept of creating your own "Internet TV station." It intrigued him to see how fast things were moving to the online realm. At first he hesitated with the idea of creating videos, but after he started it became easy. He began hearing positive feedback from the blog and Facebook readers which made the work fun and rewarding.

YouTube allowed Andy to add his videos to his own YouTube branded channel — in a sense, his own "Internet TV station." He posted his first video tutorial about a small coil-related error that often stops the washing machine from functioning. Andy shot the video on how to find out if it is the motor had been damaged and how his shop can fix it.

This video produced about 20 calls asking about his services. Andy had also promised attractive discounts on repairs if it was to be booked before a certain date and the number of calls also increased for the week. Andy's business had grown with social media marketing, and there was plenty of work to do, so he had taken the next step and hired two mechanics to help him with repairs.

The mechanics at his store were working overtime to complete the work on their hands. Andy's next YouTube videos were viewed by numerous people, and he created links on his blog, Facebook, LinkedIn and Twitter encouraging people to tune in to his YouTube account.

Andy was gaining huge popularity within just a few weeks. He once even had someone stop him in the mall and tell him they saw his show on YouTube! This was a unique experience and Andy was able to reap astounding results within a short period of time.

Andy learned that posting the video on YouTube was only the first step in getting his videos viewed. He found a tool at www.tubemogul.com that he could upload a video and with one click they would distribute it to over 10 different video distribution sites. This is important because Google loves video and will index it pretty fast, so with the URL hyperlinked properly, the videos will attract a lot of traffic.

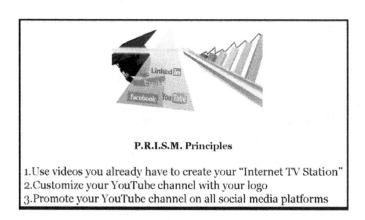

P.R.I.S.M. Principles

1.Use videos you already have to create your "Internet TV Station"
2.Customize your YouTube channel with your logo
3.Promote your YouTube channel on all social media platforms

Forums: The Original Social Media Platform

One of the oldest online interaction tools is a
forum, a place people gather to discuss specific topics.
You can easily find a forum on any topic you can imagine,
and a quick Google search turned up many opportunities
for appliance forums. Andy registered his name on
several forums and started to take part in discussions,
focusing on questions about home electrical appliances.

Every time Andy commented he tried to sound
intelligent and helpful. He worked to find a genuine
solution to each problem people faced and provided
practical and easy-to-follow tips. People started to come
back to Andy for advice whenever they had problems with
their electrical appliances. His video tutorial series and
YouTube channel became very popular when readers saw
it in his signature line.

This was not the only objective that forum
discussions fulfilled through. They were a place where
Andy got to understand the mindset of his customers. He
found out what their needs were and noted each and
every small detail he came across.

Andy used this data to provide his customers with

customized solutions, creating a sense of reliability for his brand and company. This strategy worked really well and Andy got a chance to learn market trends and things that really attracted his target market just from being involved in the forums.

He also uncovered an astounding fact: It is not always the cheaper-priced products that sell. It is actually the brand and reputation that sells. So, he knew that the marketing plan set up by Parker was highly effective in providing him with an insight into the entire social media arena and its vast usage to a small business.

- Social media is the way to realize a quicker and effective marketing plan.

- Social media can help in branding and Blogging is one of the most effective ways to grab attention from your target markets.

- Social networking sites can be a very effective way to reach your target market and learn about customer behavior.

- Social networking sites like Facebook are known

throughout the world and acts as an information hub.

- A great advantage with social networking is the ease of connecting with people from your target market.

- Forums are mini focus groups, letting companies study the needs and requirements of the customer.

- Video uploading social sites like YouTube provide a great opportunity for entrepreneurs to spread information on a particular niche.

"Shiny Object Syndrome"
Keep From Drowning in the Social Media Wave

Most small business owners have the habit of getting lost or distracted by too many ideas and opportunities around them. They tend to run after each idea or latest technology that can help their business and ultimately lose focus on their main objective. It's and issue of taking on too much, and business owners often fail to complete everything, leaving projects partially done. There are dozens and dozens of other social media platforms to sign up for and participate in. But at some point you just need to focus on a balanced approach.

This loss of focus is often referred to as the "Shiny Object Syndrome." Your attention is drawn away by a newer and more exciting item. It's a problem that is causing small businesses to lose a lot of money as well as time on non-productive activities.

Marketing plans designed to exploit social media cause people to go overboard with their efforts and in the process become spread too thin while attempting to build buzz about their business. Most people are spending hours on their laptops and computers while tweeting and making comments. This is a great option as long as one sticks to one particular platform. But as soon as people see something new, they desert their plan and never return to the initial platform. They are neither able to get the best out of any of the systems because they lack focus.

Marketing techniques, like the use of social media, need to take into consideration the bigger picture. It's very easy for us to jump at the sight of new marketing ideas. We even start off learning with great enthusiasm and implement them without even determining their specific use to the business.

119

When you work on your plan or have any ideas, stick to it until it's finished. Get this glued into your brain and business. Stick to your ideas until they're finished before moving on to the next one.

P.R.I.S.M. Principles

1. Do you have the time and energy to put into the social media marketing plan for a consistent period of time? Social media campaigns need regular maintenance and if you are not sure whether you have the time, then it is better to slowly start the process so that you can handle the extra tasks.
2. Focus: Work off of a to-do list and block out times in your schedule to work on your social media networking. Use a tool such as http://budurl.com/VirtualEggTimer to completely focus your attention and get dramatically more done in less time.
3. There is no point in being caught up by social media and lose sight of your larger goals. You are there to help and attract people to your business.

Still, though, you may find yourself overwhelmed and the only way around this is to outsource your marketing tactics to a marketing consulting company. This way you can stay focused on what is important to moving your business forward.

The social media marketing plan proved to be a salvation for Andy's business and it wasn't long before he was turning in record revenues and business was booming. He was handling more and more customers at his shop during the day while being busy with his social media campaigns at other times.

Andy Jr. was busy attending his classes while taking a few responsibilities in his father's business. Most of the time Andy Jr. was busy with his friends and at night worked on Facebook, LinkedIn and Twitter to help solve customer questions whenever required.

Each of Andy's family members played an active role in the business. But soon it was taking over their quality family time that Ann missed so much. Ann never expected that Andy's love for his business would make him forget about their anniversary or even the good night kiss that he had made a habit for so many years. Pressure to handle all facets of the business took over Andy's family life. The worst part was that he couldn't comprehend how buried he was, and it was making him stressed all the time.

At their next meeting Parker asked, "Andy, is the volume of work you've got now manageable for you and your family?"

"Actually, I am taking on too much stress and I've been thinking about your idea to hire a marketing professional. Even when I do find someone I'm not sure that they will provide me with the right kind of support within my budget. I received immense help from you and SBDC but I don't know if I can trust others the way I trust you".

Parker said, "There are a lot of people who grow their businesses using social media just like you. But when you lose your focus on the primary purpose — repairing appliances — then it might be time to bring in outside help and outsource marketing so you can take on a supervisory role. This not only allows you to take the business to newer heights but also provides an opportunity to spend time with your family."

"Tell me something, how many days in the past two months have you gone out to a movie or a party with your family?" Parker asked.

"None, as far as I can remember," Andy answered, surprised at what he said. He went silent for a minute. But Andy was still in doubt about hiring a marketing professional.

"I can't trust anybody to handle the entire job of looking after my social media campaign," Andy blurted.

"OK, think of it like this: You have learned an enormous amount of strategy and tactics in integrating social media into your marketing plan. So tasks such as creating articles, posting to your blog and marketing your videos and articles online are the things that take up so much of your time, correct?"

Andy nodded.

Parker continued, "So, what if you outsourced all of the time-consuming tasks and concentrated your efforts on answering technical questions from customers and prospects and then maintained personal connections on specific social media platforms to keep the personal touch? This way, a marketing consultant could take your marketing efforts to the next level with high-level tactics while you maintain the personal touch."

Andy replied, "Parker, I think it's time to take your advice once again. Can you can recommend someone for me to work with so I can get my life back in balance?"

"Great decision, Andy, I'm proud of you. I have just the thing you need. It's a 'Virtual Marketing Department' for small businesses that cannot afford to hire a full-time marketing director. I'm sure you looked into the costs involved — salary, insurance, workers compensation, benefits, computer equipment, training — and seen that the total cost could run easily over $50,000 a year."

"Yes," Andy exclaimed. "I did go down that thought process recently, I just can't afford that at all."

"Don't worry", Parker assured him, "You'll find that this will be the solution you are looking for... and at far lower cost than you would imagine."

Two months later...

Andy hired the firm Parker recommended to operate as his "Virtual Marketing Department" and Andy began returning early from his store to spend quality time with his family. He returned to his old self and saw how happy his family was to have him around more often.

At times Andy reflects on his experience and credits Parker with helping him realize both the value and balance of passion and family. He was nothing less than a miracle in his life. Andy knows his business would not have taken off if not for his support team at home as well.

Andy's wife, Ann, and his children, Abigail and Andy Jr., have supported him through all the ups and downs.

And Andy didn't forget Carl, who first informed him about the SBDC seminar. Andy was proud of himself for keeping hope and making it big in the world of small business. In fact, taking into consideration all Andy learned from Parker, and the tremendous increase in revenues his social media marketing plan has brought in, it's nothing short of a salvation to his business.

NOTES:

Chapter 3
Applying the Story

Small business owners often face problems with branding and marketing just like Andy did, but all are not as lucky as he was to be guided by someone like Parker. Marketing is a fast-changing arena where the core strategies still are customer focused, but so many things get in the way while keeping the business running, that it's very difficult to stay consistent with marketing.

Social media is an effective tool to analyze, as well as reach out to, customers and target audiences. The fast-changing customer behavior and market trends would take much longer through conventional methods, but with social media tools this process is expedited.

P.R.I.S.M. Principles

1. Focus on what is important to your target audience
2. Find out what they like about your product or services
3. Strengthen your competitive advantage to stand out from your competitors

This entire process can be achieved through the use of social media — what we saw Parker and Andy discover together.

Small businesses need to widen their reach and need a medium to do so. Newspapers, radio and television are good media to achieve this, but they can be expensive for small businesses and have lost their effectiveness in recent years. Earlier, people did not have any alternatives, but with the power of social media, it has become easy for people to share their ideas and messages to a larger crowd.

Social media's power is incomparable to other

marketing outlets. Integrating a blog with platforms like Facebook, Twitter, LinkedIn, and forums offer a huge return on your investment of time and extend your branding beyond your community.

Going through this book we learned that there is always hope for your business, it only requires courage, conviction and perseverance to reach out to the people that can help you. I hope *The P.R.I.S.M. Salvation* has clearly explained that a solid social media marketing system relies on knowing the basics a traditional marketing plan.

Now that you understand how to use social media for the growth of your small business there's no stopping your success.

Easy Initial Action Steps:

1. Set up profiles on Facebook and LinkedIn and Twitter.

2. Get a web designer to set up a WordPress blog that you host on your own server to give you more marketing power. Look at

hosting services such as www.smallbusinessbloghosting.com

3. Begin educating your audience with helpful topics on your services and encourage interaction with comments.

Mike's Bold Prediction

Social media will continue to grow more and more confusing with the explosion of "new and improved" social media networking sites being created.

1. The ONLY way to succeed in social media marketing for your business is to choose 2-3 social media platforms to stay consistent with.
2. YOU WILL FAIL ... if you cannot find a way to SIMPLIFY your social media activities.
3. The solution is "The Social Media Dashboard"-1-Click access to simplify your social media marketing.

Chapter 4
Integrating an MBA-Level Marketing Strategy with Social Media

Marketing Mix

Marketing decisions generally fall into the following categories:

- Product: The company's goods and services

- Price: At what level of cost the products and services are sold

- Place: Where customer accesses your products and services

- Promotion: How and where you communicate your marketing message to your target audience

These are known as the "4 Ps of Marketing" and became popular after Neil H. Borden published his 1964 article, "The Concept of the Marketing Mix". Social media marketing touches on a few of these points but it's true power is on "Promotion." By utilizing a solid social media campaign you can reduce your overall expense of marketing and then become more price-competitive. By offering your products and services online you give customers a convenient transaction venue while still promoting your business. A British marketing resource, MMC Learning, states: (*What is IMC?*) "Integrated Marketing Communications is a simple concept. It ensures that all forms of communications and messages are carefully linked together. At its most basic level, Integrated Marketing Communications, or IMC, as we'll call it, means integrating all the promotional tools, so that they work together in harmony. Promotion is one of the Ps in the marketing mix and has its own mix of communications tools."

"All of these communication tools work better if they work together in harmony rather than in isolation. Their sum is greater than their parts — providing they speak consistently with one voice all the time, every time. Although Integrated Marketing Communications requires a lot of effort, it delivers many benefits. It can create competitive advantage, boost sales and profits while saving money, time and stress."

"IMC wraps communications around customers and helps them move through the various stages of the buying process."

"This 'Relationship Marketing' cements a bond of loyalty with customers which can protect them from the inevitable onslaught of competition. The ability to keep a customer for life is a powerful competitive advantage."

MMC Learning describes the exact opportunity that a properly designed social media marketing strategy provides. Creating relationships through interactions with your audience is vital to your business and what better way than to reach out through social media?

Integrating a variety of marketing tools into your marketing mix will give balance to your marketing efforts. What if all you ever did was advertise on a popular radio station? After a while that would get old and the effectiveness would die. Contrast that to a clearly defined marketing message delivered to your target audience through blog posts that encourage interaction. Positive or negative responses are welcomed because it gives you the chance to respond and go deeper.

How did the visitor find your blog? They saw an

article or press release online that directed them to learn more at your blog. Or they watched an online video spotlighting the key points of your business which led them to your blog which led them to your pages on Facebook, LinkedIn or Twitter. Your blog should really be a "hub" leading readers to all your social media connections so they can go deeper in conversation with you about your business.

TV advertising is being replaced with online video, radio advertising is being replaced by podcasts, newspaper advertising is being replaced with comments and connections on social networks focused on your industry. This is because the consumer's voice is so much more powerful than it has ever been. When you are looking for X, Y, or Z product and read a few comments and reviews online from people who just bought it, many times this has a powerful impact on your decision. This can be all it takes to stimulate the purchase of your product.

Another powerful concept in MBA Marketing curriculum is "positioning". According to Entrepreneur.com, positioning is "how you differentiate your product or service from that of your competitors and then determine which market niche to fill. Positioning helps establish your product's or service's identity within the eyes of the purchaser. A company's positioning strategy is affected by a number of variables related to customers' motivations and requirements, as well as by its competitors' actions." (Positioning)

The key to understand here is "in the mind of the purchaser." When you need to blow your nose, do you reach for a "tissue" or a "Kleenex?" See how "Kleenex" is positioned in your mind as a substitute for the term "tissue"?

This is how a product is positioned over time to be the obvious choice, and an Integrated Marketing Communication strategy, when done effectively, allows you to properly position yourself in front of your audience.

SWOT Analysis

One of the first things you learn in business school is about "SWOT Analysis," which is a strategic planning method used to evaluate the **S**trengths, **W**eaknesses, **O**pportunities, and **T**hreats involved in a project or in a business venture. It involves specifying the business venture or project objective and identifying internal and external factors that are favorable and unfavorable to achieving that objective. The technique is credited to Albert Humphrey, who led a convention at Stanford University in the 1960s and 1970s using data from Fortune 500 companies.

How does a SWOT Analysis relate to social media marketing? ("SWOT analysis") Consider this:

Strength: Once you discover the strengths of your products and services, you can communicate it easier to your social media networks

Weakness: If social media networking is a weakness of yours, recognize this and get better so that your reach is improved

Opportunity: There is no better way to connect and promote your products and services than social media marketing. By presenting and educating your audience with the specifics of your particular opportunity you will increase your business

Threat: Set up a social media marketing strategy so that your competitors do not do it first and threaten your revenues

These points may seem trite, but you need to realize that you can run your social media strategy, as well as any project in your business, through this model to gain specific perspectives for success.

The P.R.I.S.M. Salvation

- **P**owerful

- **R**elationships

- **I**ntegrating

- **S**ocial

- **M**edia

Appendix:
Parker's P.R.I.S.M Principles

This appendix is designed as a reference to help you implement the principles and concepts in *The P.R.I.S.M. Salvation*. The appendix contains:

1. Facebook Strategies

2. 50 Powerful LinkedIn Tactics

3. 50 Powerful Twitter Tactics

4. 50 Powerful YouTube Tactics

5. Social Media Industry Research and Statistics

Facebook Strategies

www.facebook.com

A lot of people undermine the power of Facebook as a marketing tool and relate to it as nothing but a waste of time. That might be true of people who use it for tracing high school classmates or for playing brainless video games. But what about book authors who use Facebook to host virtual release parties? What about non-governmental organizations who raise massive donations for charitable causes?

The easiest way to make a Facebook profile work for you is by linking it back to your main website, online store, or wherever you promote your product from. But there are other ways as well.

A fan page is a webpage that can be created by anyone. It is a method of getting feedback from other enthusiasts or non-enthusiasts regarding a particular subject. Facebook has recently changed the term for joining a page. Previously it was called, becoming a "fan" of the page, but now you ask people to "like" your page.

Book authors use fan pages to promote a novel they liked or their own novel and invite opinions of other people. Business owners can follow in their footsteps and import blog posts with the notes application to keep your fans updated.

Or you may make a group page on Facebook to gather like-minded visitors. This can also help in marketing your brand as you can promote yourself as an industry expert.

Say you enjoy talking about gourmet food and act as a food critic for a hobby. Via the group page you can advise visitors on which restaurants to visit for a particular cuisine and the details of new restaurants that recently opened in your city.

Facebook's newsfeed has an important application as well. It serves as an instant message board for all kinds of important announcements that you may need to make regarding a new product, a sale, or service. It is also extremely helpful in connecting with your customers. Just post the details of all points of sale and the relevant URLs and see the increase in click-through traffic.

A powerful strategy is to create a Welcome tab that page visitors see first which has high-quality graphics encouraging them to "like" your page. It's also very critical to include an opt-in box to offer something of value to the visitor to request. This collects their email address so that you can communicate with them in the future by email. Look at companies like www.emailfollowupservice.com where all features of an email follow-up campaign are provided at a low cost.

50 Powerful LinkedIn Tactics

www.linkedin.com

1. Check the Expertise Requests option in your profile

2. Complete your profile as thoroughly as possible, and include interests, a picture, and business information

3. Connect with as many business associates as you can, since they will help you to network with like-minded individuals and companies

4. Learn from others and gain new knowledge, so you can become an expert in other subjects and topics

5. Ask questions

6. Answer questions and use your knowledge to your advantage by offering thorough and expert

answers — you'll gain other users' confidence

7. Check your home page on LinkedIn fairly often as it contains industry updates, news, and postings from associates

8. On company profiles, take notice of the top five most popular profiles which are displayed on the home page since it will show others who you associate with (also be aware of who your top five are)

9. Choose the top five who will link back to you, so there is a reciprocal benefit

10. Be sure to explain your work experience in as much detail as possible. Don't just list employers or experience, but instead expand upon it by showing others what you've done in detail

11. Comment in the discussion forums as much as you can so your profile gets noticed

12. Update your status with useful content and information as much as possible

13. Implement keywords in both your profile and your content, so that your information comes up in search engine results

14. Do not forget to include your LinkedIn profile link in other places like Twitter, Facebook, and other social media websites

15. LinkedIn is also a useful employment tool, so if you're hiring, use it to find good employees

16. Customize your buttons to make your profile look more professional and give you more control

17. Include your skills and specialties and be sure to expand upon your current business

18. Include your company's website somewhere on your profile

19. Have a plan in place when you begin to build your network, otherwise you may end up getting contacts you don't want, and not enough of the ones you do

20. Do not just be friends with people because they ask you to. It looks a little odd for a professional member to be friend with their partying buddies from college. Leave the casual online friendships to Facebook

21. Look at network statistics to see what is going on with your account and the progress you're making

22. Keep in mind the number of characters in profile fields are limited, so you may want to do a few practice runs first before publishing everything

23. Include past education and past companies and experience, not just your current business or company

24. Customize your public profile's URL so it's easier to link this to other pages and people will remember it much better

25. Utilize the reference check tool to find out how long someone worked for a company and much more

26. Ask others within the community for advice. Since this site was designed for networking, people are usually more than willing to answer questions and give help

27. Use the site to help get a much clearer picture of your competition

28. Compliment others and give them praise when you're speaking to them, so that they reciprocate. It makes both of your profiles look much better and can increase your exposure and ratings

29. Do not only mention what you've done, but include what you've produced. Be sure to post results from your actions and include facts and figures if possible

30. Use numbers and show people percentages and real numbers that back up the claims of your success

31. The top of your summary is what visitors see first so be certain you're including the most vital information here

32. Utilize the answers tool as an opportunity to show off you expertise

33. If you're in need of a graphic designer, web hosting provider, or any other service, LinkedIn has its own services area where you can trade with others who are among the trusted network

34. Use your LinkedIn page link in your blog, and favorite business resources

35. Try to become a recommended service or company by establishing a good reputation. People will flock more toward ones that have the "recommended" status

36. Enable the "show website" feature in your profile

37. Make sure the full view and websites options are also checked so that the information in your profile is public

38. LinkedIn is mostly designed for targeted marketing, so be as specific as you can when you choose your industry and expertise

39. Use the website as a tool to make connections within your business niche, and then expand upon those connections on other social media sites

40. Be willing to work at building your network; it takes time to get a lot of solid connections

41. Make use of the option to be indexed so your information appears on Google and other search engines' results

42. Use the Q&A feature to ask others their opinion of your website, product, and promotion tactics

43. Feel free to introduce yourself to other members. Don't always wait for others to approach you

44. Ask others to recommend you if they have had experience with you

45. Think of LinkedIn as your "home base" for all of your professional networking

46. Edit your profile often and rearrange things as needed, so you are always up to date and content is refreshed

47. Use the groups feature to meet others, post feedback, and get a feel for what other companies are up to

48. Start your network base with people you know and trust, and build from there

49. Be as professional as possible at all times

50. Always be aware of spelling and grammar

50 Powerful Twitter Tactics

www.twitter.com

1.   Network with noteworthy business associates, competitors, and peers. You don't have to simply befriend every person you can that requests you or vice versa on Twitter. Instead, choose your networking buddies carefully. Look for fellow executives or business owners who work within your particular industry

2.   Then, follow their progress, look for advice, and of course, throw in your own two cents. By following people who are in the same line of work as you, you'll get an insider's look at how their successes compare to yours

3.   Update your audience fairly regularly, but don't overload them. A lot of people are most likely interested in what you have to say, otherwise they probably wouldn't have added you to begin with. On the other hand, you don't want to overload people so much that the feel of your Twitter site feels "spammy" and they turn away.

Try to maintain the balance between necessary updating and significant updates

4. Use Twitterfeed.com to help people stay updated. Twitterfeed automatically updates your followers without the need to check your page too often

5. Use Twitter at conferences and trade shows. When you're out and about networking in the *real* world, don't forget to use Twitter as an opportunity to update your customers and peers on what you're seeing and doing. This shows them that you're being proactive and it's a lot of fun as well

6. You can tell them some funny things you might be seeing at the trade show, or maybe inform them of an interesting vendor you've hooked up with. By sharing experiences as you go, you're garnering more interest in what is happening with your business

7. Don't forget that Twitter, like any virtual conversation, is a two-way street. Pay attention to what other members are saying, and see if

they're Twittering about you. If they are, you might want to use that as an opportunity to either thank them or make good if they posted a complaint. Remember that you're never 100 percent safe from someone who might try to talk negatively about you, your website, or anything else on Twitter. Be sure to use this to your advantage in a diplomatic way

8. Display your Twitter profile on business cards, your website, and in email signatures. Remind people in other ways that you're on Twitter. Some clients and customers might not know this until you pass the information along. Get a nice snapshot of your Twitter home page and then display it along with a link to the Twitter page on your company's website

9. Make Twitter another home hub. Use Twitter to display your business growth, charts, statistics, and other factual data. This way, people who prefer to watch what's happening with you on Twitter have the same basic information and access as those who usually just visit your website

10. Promote events to your followers. This can be anything from an appearance at a trade show to a huge seasonal sale or a launching of a new product. Always keep Twitter in mind when it comes to these updates, and remember that it can reach a lot more people than just your email subscribers

11. Filter your traffic to other places. You can use Twitter to steer people to other resources such as your blog or website. The exchange of information through Twitter can go both ways. It's a good way to get others moving to different resources that you have available that they might not know about

12. Find a cool background template that says who you are as company. Twitter allows users to customize the look of their home page. Use something individual and creative as your Twitter page. This can be the same graphics you use on your website, a company logo, or something you've customized just for Twitter. No matter what it is, make sure it's appealing to the eyes and does not look too busy

13. Why email when you can tweet? Don't send short and sweet emails to your subscribers. Most people who sign up for emails from companies expect a monthly and at least weekly update that is chock full of information. They don't want to open a short email with not much to go on. Save this for Twitter, where people hunger for short sentences and blurbs. Then, you can compile all of these over the span of a month or so into one email for the others

14. Use a cool "follow me" graphic. There are now hundreds of different follow me graphics to choose from that will grab peoples' attention. You can even customize your graphic if you want to, so people will see something distinctive about your page. Just like the template, the follow me graphics get you notice and entice people to want more information, so make sure this graphic is done well

15. Remember that Twitter is a social site and it's got more of a casual feel. Make sure the posts are generally light, with a touch of humor otherwise you might lose your core audience. The purpose of following others on Twitter is so that it's entertaining. If you post too serious or heavy

posts, it might turn some readers off

16.   Sub-divide your Twitter page. You don't have to
      have just one company page. Instead, try to come
      up with a page for each of your staff. This way,
      your customers get to know others on the team.
      It also adds a bit of diversity to the business, and
      gives customers a cast of characters to follow
      instead of a faceless, nameless company. It also
      entices people to follow more so they stay
      connected to both you and your business

17.   Incorporate video into your Twitter page. Twitter
      now allows for multimedia additions and video
      plug-ins on your page. This makes it more
      exciting, and people will want to follow your
      postings more closely if there's video included

18.   Divide and conquer. You can actually separate
      your followers into different groups. This is
      actually quite useful, especially if some people
      are customers, some are peers, some are
      competitors, and some are personal contacts.
      This way, you only update the people who care
      about certain things with particular tweets, while
      others don't have to see those, and vice versa. It's

a good way to hone in on your audience's interests

19. iTunes, iPhones, and Twitter: There are plenty of new tools available right now that incorporated into Apple's applications. This makes your Twitter updates available to busy people who are on the go, and for people who access your page solely on their iPhones

20. It's not just for iPhones any more: Aside from the iPhone specific applications, there are plenty of other mobile Twitter apps out there. Not only can your users download these apps and use them on their cell phones, but you can do the same and follow your friends as well

21. Inform your customers of stock status. Twitter also has tons of great features and plug-ins that will notify your customers when certain items you carry are in stock or go on sale. This also allows you to get a jump start on your suppliers and what they are offering for you

22. Map it out. Google Maps and many other map websites now integrate with Twitter. This can be

fun to show your followers where you're traveling, or just to show them where your business is located. It's also handy so that you can find posters and look up where they are located

23. Twitter is a great way to get insight into other blogs such as Digg and other related sources. This can be a good way to not only find other peoples' blogs, but link to them and inform other people about their content. By doing a search you can find tons of great blogs to link to from Twitter

24. Followers respond to contests on Twitter. Host an impromptu giveaway contest every day, every week, monthly, whatever you choose. It's a great way to get all of your followers to stay interested and engaged, and freebies are always a guarantee of new contacts

25. Ask for feedback. Don't just tell everyone what you're doing via Twitter, try to ask everyone for their opinion or feedback. It's a good way to start a dialogue and open up a forum for new suggestions and changes that can be made

26. Colors matter. Think about the color scheme of your Twitter page, and try to make it appealing and something that will fit your business' niche. For example, a NASCAR Twitter page wouldn't use a pink and red color scheme. Choose colors that fit your message and your style

27. Fonts are important, too. The fonts you use for the main Twitter page should also fit the theme of the business or page

28. Make Twitter followers feel special by offering "Twitter followers only" specials and coupons. This encourages new purchases as well as new followers

29. Offer more than just Twitter. If you're so inclined, let people know they can contact you outside of Twitter via email, text, or even phone. Open up the lines of communication

30. Use behind the scene tools. Don't forget to look at metrics and what people click on, and from where. This is definitely an invaluable tool

31. Get into a routine — a Twitter rhythm — and then stick with it. Once you get into the flow of posting, your readers will stick with you

32. Participate as much as possible. Contribute, and be a part of others' Twitter pages as well. Don't just stand in the shadows, or you might lose followers

33. Mix it up. Don't just use Twitter as a promotional site. Try to keep a dialogue going, let people know what's happening, and other things aside from over-promotion

34. Form a partnership with your fellow tweeters. Come up with a network within a network, and you'll be amazed at the results

35. Realize there are other avenues, and then expand on them. While Twitter is great, don't neglect your other social media sites, blogs, or your own website

36. Take out the trash. You can always "unfollow" people who are not posting positive comments,

other companies who spam you, or "junk" Twitter friends. Don't be afraid to clean house every once in a while

37. Future tweets reap sweet treats. You can now use tools that allow you to type up your tweets in advance so you can plan ahead, and then they will post to your account when you're ready

38. Automated tweets can help you prioritize. There are tools where you can select certain topics or sub-topics for notification, so that the topics important to you will be delivered daily, or however you like

39. Use the advanced search to your benefit. Twitter has advanced search options, so you can really find the niche poster or specified topic that you're interested in

40. Never mention a resource without linking if at all possible, this way people trust your opinions because they're backed up with real links

41. Try not to abbreviate too much. While Twitter

only allows 140 characters and that can be tough to express yourself, try to avoid too many abbreviations

42. Be as thorough as you can when explaining who you are, what your company does, and what you have to offer

43. Stay away from arguments and foul language. Some people may get obnoxious or belligerent on Twitter. Avoid arguments by ignoring them or unfollowing them

44. Don't be boring. Keep your posts fresh, fun, and interesting

45. Counts don't count. Do not worry about how many followers you have. This can distract you from the quality of your posts

46. Refuse spammers. Keep spammers and spam emailers out of your Twitter feed or else they can ruin your page

47. Ask and ye shall receive. Don't be afraid to ask

others to retweet your tweets, or to link you to their blogs. Most people will oblige if you just ask

48. Open up to your audience. Try to loosen up and have your other tweeters do the same by being honest, intimate, and real with your readers. People will really enjoy the candid postings and stay enthralled

49. Offer downloadable material. You can always offer a PDF download or other material on your Twitter page for people to look at and get more information

50. Use SEO to your advantage, and do not forget to implement important keywords in the Twitter posts

50 Powerful YouTube Tactics

www.youtube.com

1. Make your videos viral by creating them to be so fun and engaging that people feel like spreading them to as many websites as possible

2. Use other social media sites like Twitter and Digg to post your videos

3. Create well-thought-out, professional videos that are edited properly

4. Make sure the video sound is mixed and edited well so users can clearly hear it

5. Keep content funny, engaging, and informative so viewers will watch it from beginning to end

6. Try to keep the videos clean without too much controversial material

7.   Embed your logo and website into the video. You can do this with text at the end or beginning, or by including your logo or URL throughout the entire video

8.   Have goals for your YouTube videos, remembering that there are thousands of videos on the site — some with millions of hits and others with a couple hundred. Set realistic goals

9.   Make sure you have good camera and editing equipment. If you don't want to sink the money into these things, consider hiring a professional

10. Keep the resolution of the video as high as possible, so it's as clear as it can be

11. Think about overall color schemes. Some videos may record in a yellow or red hue. This can affect viewer's opinions subliminally, so try to keep the colors realistic

12. Be yourself. Do not lose sight of the purpose and mission of the video. Be yourself and loosen up when speaking

13. Remember that nothing is perfect in online videos unless you have a professional editor, so just have fun and keep the goal in mind

14. Practice before posting the final video. Do a few dry runs before taping and publishing

15. Create a series of ongoing how-to videos or stories, so users will be hooked and want to learn more

16. Do more than just talk. People don't want to sit and watch a person just talking to the camera. Make it exciting and interesting as well as fun

17. Try to limit the video to a couple of minutes if possible. After about two and a half minutes, users generally tend to lose interest and move onto something else

18. Stick to a schedule if you record a series, otherwise people will give up. Be sure to release the next ones on time

19. Have an introduction and sign off that people

will remember and stick to it. This creates a sense of branding

20. Ask for feedback from your viewers. Some people will not comment unless you ask them to

21. Assemble a cast of characters. Use other people in the videos beside yourself. Recruit friends, coworkers, and family members to be actors in the videos

22. Do not use music on your video that you do not have the rights to. This can lead to all kinds of problems, so either use your own or get permission

23. The title of the video is just as important as the content

24. Grab viewers by integrating important keywords into the title. This also helps boost the search engine results

25. Use tags in addition to the keywords, as this also gets peoples' attention

26. If people post negative comments, ignore them. By "feeding the trolls" you are encouraging their bad behavior and you might say something you regret later on

27. Use as many places as you can to embed your video, like Facebook, LinkedIn, Digg, Twitter, your home page, and many other places

28. Let your email subscribers and customers know when a new video is posted

29. Add your video to various communities and subject areas of YouTube for more exposure

30. Be sure to thank people who post positive comments or consider themselves followers of your videos

31. Be aware that not all videos you create will be a hit. It is a hit-and-miss venture, so be patient and practice making good videos

32. Write the script in advance. While impromptu videos are fun, it's really easy to mess up the

vision when you improvise

33. Use analytics tools like YouTube Insight to track your sources and hits

34. Actually use the word "video" in your title, since people usually include this word, and it will get a lot more results in the search engines. In the description start it off with: http:// then the URL to your blog or website. This will hotlink the address in Google.

35. Do not make your video an advertisement. In other words, get a point across without trying to sell something

36. Choose the thumbnail wisely. YouTube actually lets users choose their thumbnails so do it carefully and thoughtfully

37. You can delete comments, so do not hesitate to get rid of negative or rude comments under your video

38. You can release more than one video at once

39. Be real and do not try to fake out your viewers. Most people can spot a fake video or something that isn't sincere

40. Have fun and focus on fun, so you're creating something people will want to share and forward to others

41. Aside from your logo and website, include a way for people to contact you or your business via email or Twitter or Facebook page

42. Watch others and learn. By viewing other videos that are related to your business, you can get a feel for what people are doing, and what others are saying about it

43. Stick to your target audience. Don't try to branch out too far from your purpose or you could easily lose loyal followers

44. Upload webcam live videos. Have a webcam located at your office, or other location, and then upload this onto your YouTube channel. It's a fun way to get others involved in the day-to-day

operations of what you are doing

45. Make a channel and profile. This gives viewers a
     home base to look at your videos and check on
     any new ones

46. Do not use curse words or inappropriate
     language and behavior

47. Use props, costumes, and other fun things in
     your video. Fancy editing does not always make
     for the best viewing

48. Try to open each video with a small montage,
     song, or your logo, so that people easily
     recognize your business or who you are

49. Utilize TubeMogul and other sites to get your
     video exposed to other audiences

50. Specify your channel type, and have a clear sense
     of what you're offering on the channel's main
     page

NOTES:

Social Media Industry Research and Statistics

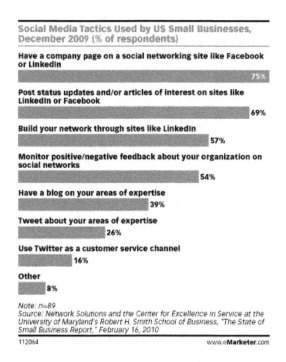

Social Media Tactics Used by US Small Businesses, December 2009 (% of respondents)

Have a company page on a social networking site like Facebook or LinkedIn — 75%

Post status updates and/or articles of interest on sites like LinkedIn or Facebook — 69%

Build your network through sites like LinkedIn — 57%

Monitor positive/negative feedback about your organization on social networks — 54%

Have a blog on your areas of expertise — 39%

Tweet about your areas of expertise — 26%

Use Twitter as a customer service channel — 16%

Other — 8%

Note: n=89
Source: Network Solutions and the Center for Excellence in Service at the University of Maryland's Robert H. Smith School of Business, "The State of Small Business Report," February 16, 2010
112064   www.eMarketer.com

From eMarketer: "According to 'The State of Small Business Report' from Network Solutions and the Center for Excellence in Service at the University of Maryland Robert H. Smith School of Business. Social media usage increased to 24 percent, from 12 percent the year before. The most common usage of social media among small business was a company page on a social networking site, followed by posting status updates.

Facebook Marketing Works

Dr. Jeff Cornwall, known for his blog "The Entrepreneurial Mind," asks just how effective social media is as marketing tools, especially for those trying to bootstrap their businesses.

New research from Utpal Dholakia and Emily Durham of Rice University takes a look at this question in the article, *One Café Chain's Facebook Experiment,* featured in the March issue of the *Harvard Business Review*. (Cornwall, 2010)

According to this study, companies that use Facebook and its fan page module to market themselves to customers can increase sales, word-of-mouth marketing and customer loyalty.

Dholakia and Durham surveyed customers of Dessert Gallery (DG), a popular Houston-based café chain. Prior to the study, DG did not have a Facebook presence.

The study, based on surveys of more than 1,700 respondents over a three-month period, found that compared with typical DG customers, the company's Facebook fans:

- Made 36 percent more visits to DG's stores each month

- Spent 45 percent more of their eating-out dollars at DG

- Spent 33 percent more at DG's stores

- Had 14-percent higher emotional attachment to the DG brand

- Had 41 percent greater psychological loyalty toward DG

According to Dholakia, the results indicate that Facebook fan pages offer an effective and low-cost way of social-media marketing.

"We must be cautious in interpreting the study's

results," Dholakia said. "The fact that only about 5 percent of the firm's 13,000 customers became Facebook fans within three months indicates that Facebook fan pages may work best as niche marketing programs targeted to customers who regularly use Facebook. Social-media marketing must be employed judiciously with other types of marketing programs."

Dholakia said Facebook marketing programs may be especially effective for iconic brands, which appear to attract a higher percentage of their customer base as Facebook fans.

To understand how marketers are using social media, it is important to use survey data to see how the market is moving. Reprinted with permission of the author, Michael A. Stelzner, this data is presented here for you. He set out to uncover the "who, what, where, when and why" of social media marketing. Nearly 900 people provided the kind of insight that previously has not existed. (Stelzner, 2009) In the full report you'll find:

- The top social media marketing questions marketers want answered

- How much time marketers are investing in social

media

- The benefits of social media

- How time invested impacts results

- The top social media tools

If you're pondering starting social media marketing, these findings will help push you over the edge.

Commonly Used Social Media Tools

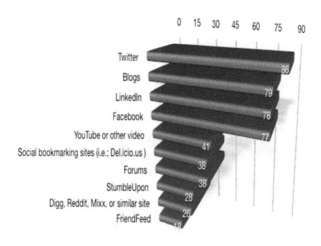

By a long shot, Twitter, blogs, LinkedIn and Facebook were the top four social media tools used by marketers, with Twitter leading the pack. All other social media platforms paled in comparison to these top four.

Owners of small businesses were more likely to use LinkedIn than employees working for a corporation. Another interesting finding was that men were significantly more likely to use YouTube or other video marketing than women (52.4 percent of all men compared to only 31.7 percent of women).

The Benefits of Social Media Marketing

The number one benefit of social media marketing is gaining the all-important eyeball. A significant 81 percent of all marketers indicated that their social media efforts have generated exposure for their businesses. Improving traffic and growing lists was the second major benefit, followed by building new partnerships.

An unexpected benefit was a rise in search engine rankings reported by more than half of all participants. As the search engine rankings improve, so will business exposure, lead generation efforts and a reduction in overall marketing expenses. About one in two marketers found social media generated qualified leads. However, only slightly more than one in three said social media marketing helped to close the business deal.

Some questions that naturally emerge from the above chart might include, "Is there a way to improve the likelihood of achieving these benefits by investing more time in social media?" and "Are those marketers who've been doing social media marketing for years gaining even better results?" The answer to these questions can be obtained in the full report from Stelzner.

Resources

- To Find a Small Business Development Center (SBDC), in your area, visit www.SBA.gov

Click "local resources" then "small business development centers."

- For a list of recommended resources to help run your business and social media campaigns more efficiently, visit:

www.ThePrismSalvation.com

Click on the Resources link. This page will be constantly updated with new and cutting-edge social media marketing tools. By signing up for email updates you will always be aware of the latest tools to succeed in your marketing.

To learn more about how a "Virtual Marketing Department benefits a small business, visit: www.MarketingHuddle.com

Services Available

- Social Media Marketing

- Blog Marketing

- Article Marketing

- Video Marketing

- SEO Website Marketing

- Marketing Strategy Consulting

For more information on the above services or to check availability to teach marketing courses through your school's online program, contact:

Mike Saunders, MBA

Mike@MarketingHuddle.com

Marketing Huddle, LLC

PO Box 746003

Denver, Co. 80003

Toll-Free: 1-888-467-6374

www.ThePrismSalvation.com

www.MarketingHuddle.com

www.VirtualMarketingProfessor.com

About The Author

Mike Saunders, MBA has over 18 years experience in sales and marketing and has been a top producer earning several awards and recognitions including being recognized as the No. 1 Sales Producer in the Country two years in a row for a national financial institution.

Through his MBA coursework, Mike created the Marketing Huddle, a marketing consulting firm focusing on helping small business owners use the latest cutting-edge marketing tools and systems to increase business.

His areas of expertise include:

1. Coaching and consulting clients as a Virtual Marketing Department with both strategy and implementation.

2. Marketing consultant with the Denver Small Business Development Center (SBDC)

3. Adjunct Marketing Professor for select colleges and universities

Mike is passionate about online learning and with his MBA and 18 graduate hours in marketing, he works as a "Virtual Marketing Professor," teaching marketing classes for colleges and universities through their online learning departments.

Mike has been married for 13 years and has three daughters and a son. He enjoys spending time at his family's cabin in the mountains of Colorado, hiking and riding ATVs, and enjoys playing acoustic guitar in the College and Career Sunday School class he teaches at church.

References

Cornwall, J. (2010). *Evidence that Facebook works as marketing tool*. USA: Belmont University. Retrieved from http://www.drjeffcornwall.com/2010/03/evidence-that-facebook-works-a.html

Edelman. (2006). *Annual trust barometer*. USA. Retrieved from http://www.edelman.com/image/insights/content/FullSupplement.pdf

Smith, J. (2009). *Fastest growing demographic on facebook: Women over 55*. USA: Inside Facebook. Retrieved from http://www.insidefacebook.com/2009/02/02/fastest-growing-demographic-on-facebook-women-over-55/

Godin, S. (2007). *Meatball sundae*. USA: Penguin Group.

Nielsen, J. (2006). *Participation Inequality:encouraging more users to contribute*. USA: useit.com. Retrieved from http://www.useit.com/alertbox/participation_inequality.html

Positioning. USA: Entrepreneur. Retrieved from http://www.entrepreneur.com/encyclopedia/term/82364.html

Silverthorne, S. (2009). *PR nightmare: United Airlines*

breaks guitars. USA: BNET. Retrieved from
http://blogs.bnet.com/harvard/?p=3130

Stelzner, M. (2009). *Social media marketing industry report*. USA: Whitepaper Source. Retrieved from
http://www.whitepapersource.com/socialmediam
arketing

SWOT analysis. USA: Wikipedia. Retrieved from
http://en.wikipedia.org/wiki/SWOT_analysis

Brill, E. (2006). *The bottom line on blogging*. USA:
Kansas City Star. Retrieved from
http://blogs.zdnet.com/Brill/?p=223

What is IMC? USA: MMC Learning. Retrieved from
http://www.multimediamarketing.com/mkc/mar
ketingcommunications/

www.ingramcontent.com/pod-product-compliance
Lightning Source LLC
Chambersburg PA
CBHW071152050326
40689CB00011B/2077